CHICAGO DAILY
SUN  TIMES
THE PICTURE NEWSPAPER

SPORT
SPECIAL

REAL CHICAGO SPORTS

PHOTOGRAPHS FROM THE FILES OF THE CHICAGO SUN-TIMES

INTRODUCTION BY RICK TELANDER

RICHARD CAHAN
MICHAEL WILLIAMS
NEAL SAMORS

A CITYFILES PRESS BOOK

CONTENTS

INTRODUCTION RICK TELANDER

I love photographs. Even with all the gadgetry of modern times—videos, digitalized animation, streaming music and the virtual reality googles that the computer can bring us—I love still photos most. Their magic reigns. It is why, if I have any tasks ahead, I am reluctant to open the covers of my family photo albums. It is why I hesitate to peek at picture magazines. Open them for a moment, and time runs away. Where did the afternoon go?

The overarching theme of this book is Chicago sports. But its underlying theme is photography. The beauty and clarity of these prints are obvious. The skill of these photographers is apparent. This is a book filled with moments in time—frozen and laid out so we can simply look at them. Photographs are a gift.

Take the photo on Page 113, of Northwestern football coach Ara Parseghian celebrating a big play at Dyche Stadium. The toe of Parseghian's lightly blurred left shoe is perhaps one inch off the ground, and it was precisely like that for a micro-fraction of a second. But it was caught on film, and it will never change. Just behind Ara is assistant coach Alex Agase, clearly second in command, turning to the troops and letting his players know that he's thrilled, too. Again, frozen for all time. (By the way, I know it's Agase, even though his face is partly hidden by his right hand, because I recognize the angular noggin of the man who would be my coach at Northwestern several years after Parseghian left for Notre Dame.) Here's the point: A person could look at this photo for hours, studying nuances, and not be sated.

When I worked at *Sports Illustrated*, I once asked the managing editor why he thought the magazine was so successful even though all it offered in fast-moving times were old-fashioned words and old-fashioned photographs. Mainly, I meant the photographs. "It's the savor factor," he replied. People, he explained, like to take their time perusing things they may already have seen or may only have heard about. And the frozen nature of photographs means the scene can never change. Only one's perception changes. Film and video may have sound and movement, but photographs are wildly more provocative.

As you go through this book, see if you don't find yourself amused, startled, captivated, thrilled and mystified. Chicago has had enough sports stars and sports characters and sports moments to fill ten of these collections. But these are the best photos, the most rewarding. Bronko Nagurski, George Mikan, Luke Appling, Dick Butkus, Ernie Banks, Ray Meyer, Mike Ditka,

Ryne Sandberg—they're all here. So are a lot of unknown athletes—passersby on the bigger stage. Even a fellow like "Machine Gun" Jack McGurn takes a bow at a local bowling alley. Bowling is a sport, is it not? Trouble is, Jack's dead. He was shot by Chicago bad guys. It may be proof of the savor factor that I have looked at that photo so many times that I have come to enjoy the prone man's casual posture, his spats, the way the blood has not soiled his white shirt, the spittoon in the corner, the trio of bowling balls perched at the end of the return, just above his head, waiting—forever—for the mobster to stand up, dry his hands on the towel and get rolling. I appreciate that even more because I know the photographer captured it on the fly. And I know he was secure enough in his craft to know that the details, the things to ponder, would be there when his negative underwent its mystical transformation in the darkroom.

Then, too, we meet sports heroes who merely passed through Chicago, leaving their marks. They include Jim Thorpe, Jake LaMotta, Willie Shoemaker and young Jack Nicklaus, all captured here. The Bulls, Bears, Cubs, White Sox, and Blackhawks all are represented in their successes (why do they seem so rare?) and their failures (why do they seem so common?). Mostly, though, the joy is in here: Ron Santo clicking his heels, Randy Hundley being adored, the 1963 Loyola basketball team posing with its NCAA championship trophy.

The fact that these photos are black-and-white only accentuates their artistry. Their lines seem more dramatic, the shadings more arresting, the patterns more revealing than true-to-life color. Yet, as authentic as these photos are, as close to the truth as they dance, they are still canvasses of creativity and imagination based on angle, lighting, cropping, equipment, and the whimsy of the men and women who pushed the buttons at those moments. What a wonderful bit of technological pizzazz to bring to the world of sport! Photography has delivered frozen jumpshots, suspended punches and fixed expressions that are never seen by the sporting crowd. The walls of my room as a kid were plastered with sports photos. So are the walls of my office today.

Let's open this album and savor these photos. And forget about the clock for awhile.

Rick Telander is a sports columnist for the Chicago Sun-Times.

RED SOX OUTFIELDER TED WILLIAMS CHECKS THE COLUMN HE WROTE FOR THE CHICAGO SUN-TIMES ON MAY 22, 1950, AT COMISKEY PARK. (PHOTO BY JOE KORDICK.)

CHICAGO SUN-TIMES PHOTOGRAPHER MICKEY RITO PIVOTS THE PAPER'S "BIG BERTHA" CAMERA AT WRIGLEY FIELD IN THE 1950S. THE CAMERA HAD A TELESCOPIC LENS TO GET CLOSE TO THE ACTION.

SPORTS AND THE CITY RICHARD CAHAN

Ernie Banks arrived at the *Chicago Sun-Times* office unannounced. He came with a request. He asked to see photographs that had been taken of him during his 19-year career as a Cub.

"I remember the cheers," he said, "but I don't remember what it all looked like." As he settled onto a hard chair in the newspaper's photo department, Banks slowly opened the file folders containing hundreds of pictures showing him after his arrival in Chicago. A 1958 picture has him at home, admiring his Most Valuable Player trophy. Another photo shows him playing catch with his twin sons. One picture has Ernie with his father. The caption on back, written by a photographer, reads, "Proudest dad in town is Eddie Banks as he examines son Ernie's war club."

Banks smiled as he looked at the pictures, often stopping to tell the stories behind them. The photographs in the *Sun-Times'* files were his record, his scrapbook. Of triumphs and defeats. Of good times and bad. They also form a scrapbook of Chicago, and of Chicago's great love—sports.

Sports tell us who we are and who we were. Some of these photos—of Depression-era dance marathons, Loop parades during World War II and American flags on display after September 11—tell us about our times. Some of the photos—of South Side smelt fishing and Lake Michigan sailing—tell us about our place. Chicago is the backdrop here. Look through the arches of Comiskey Park, or past the ivy-covered walls of Wrigley Field, and you will see a city in love with sports. We long for spring training, ache for summer night games and revel in Bears' weather. For Chicago is a sports town like no other.

We are a town of lovable losers. And since Michael Jordan, we're a trophy town. The hard-nosed Bears, who battle in the black-and-blue division, have long symbolized Chicago's grit and grind. We are Dick Butkus; we are Mike Singletary. When we bust a tooth, we are Bobby Hull. We are, in the words of Mike Ditka, Grabowskis, not Smiths. And we are a town split in half. The North Side belongs to the Cubs; the South Side belongs to the White Sox. Violate that rule and life seems out of whack.

The photo archive of the *Chicago Sun-Times* consists of hundreds of thousands of prints and negatives. The archive generally goes back to 1929, the year that the *Chicago Daily Times* published its first edition. The Times was to be Chicago's answer to the *New York Daily News*. It was billed as Chicago's Picture Newspaper. As Chicago's only major tabloid during the 1930s and '40s, the *Times* was brawny and bold and fun. It made Chicago laugh; it made Chicago mad. Its front page often was dominated by one picture and one headline. When Dizzy Dean took the mound in the 1938 World Series, the *Times* ran a huge cutout mug shot of the pitcher with the front-page headline "Do It Diz!" This was the conscience of Chicago.

Sports were a key part of the *Times* because sports drove the daily lives of its readers. Before the age of television and computers, people depended on newspapers for all their sports news. Games were so important to Chicagoans that the afternoon papers, like the *Chicago Daily News*, would run sports extras wrapping around the main front section. These extras would report on major league games as they were being played—with partial line scores and box scores.

ONE OF THE FIRST SUN-TIMES PHOTOS OF "MR. CUB," TAKEN SEPTEMBER 15, 1953, TWO DAYS BEFORE HIS MAJOR LEAGUE DEBUT.

THE CUBS TAKE ON THE PHILADELPHIA ATHLETICS IN GAME 2 OF THE WORLD SERIES ON SEPTEMBER 9, 1929. THE CHICAGO TIMES WAS FOUNDED SIX DAYS EARLIER.

WHITE SOX CATCHER SHERM LOLLAR BEFORE A GAME IN THE 1959 CHAMPION-SHIP SEASON. THE PHOTO WAS TITLED "THE MAN IN THE IRON MASK."

Marshall Field III, grandson of the founder of the Marshall Field's department store, created the *Chicago Sun* on December 4, 1941, three days before Pearl Harbor. Field wanted a paper to counterbalance the isolationist, conservative *Chicago Tribune*. In 1947, he bought the *Daily Times*, and announced that both papers would be published as tabloids on the *Times'* presses. Field first attempted to run both papers separately, but soon he combined the Sunday papers to produce the *Chicago Sun & Times*, and he combined both daily papers in 1948. The paper was called the *Chicago Sun-Times*.

When the papers merged, so merged the photography staffs and the photo archives. They were consolidated in the main office of the new *Sun-Times* at 211 West Wacker Drive. There they stayed until 1957, when the paper and the archives were moved to the new Sun-Times Building at 401 North Wabash Avenue.

In 1959, Marshall Field IV purchased the *Chicago Daily News* and moved the paper to the Sun-Times Building. Most of the *Daily News'* negatives—glass-plates, nitrate and plastic film dating back to the early 1900s—are maintained at the Chicago Historical Society. Prints from the *Daily News* archives and some negatives are kept with the *Sun-Times* photo archive at 350 North Orleans Street.

Sports continue to be key at the *Sun-Times*. The paper has long been known for its detailed sports coverage. For many Chicagoans, the paper's front page is the back page—the sports section. And when crucial games are played—such as baseball, football or basketball playoffs—the *Sun-Times* goes back to the *Daily News'* tradition of sports extras, wrapping the main paper with a special sports section.

Photos, of course, are at the heart of that coverage.

Hardly a team takes the field when a *Sun-Times* photographer is not present. For 75 years, photographers have shoved to the front of stadiums because it was their job to capture the cigar-smoke atmosphere and Cracker Jack feel of Chicago sports. Covered in plastic on rain-slick nights at Soldier Field, bundled in layers on opening days at Wrigley Field and Comiskey Park, and pushed against the glass at Chicago Stadium, *Sun-Times* photographers take direct, in-your-face photos for the not-so-lucky fans who are up in the grandstands or at home.

Were you there when the Bears intercepted five passes in the 1963 NFL Championship game? Were you there when the Blackhawks won their first regular-season championship, or when Michael Jordan took off from the free-throw line in the slam-dunk contest before the 1988 All-Star Game?

The *Sun-Times* was.

Much has changed since the *Times* photographers used pigeons to fly negatives back from the ballparks. Photographers in the '30s used Speed Graphic cameras with 4-by-5-inch negatives to cover sporting events. Film was slow, which means that action was hard to capture, so they often returned to the office with portraits of the stars of the day. Stadium lighting and faster film made action easier to catch during the '40s and '50s, but photographers usually went to games armed only with a dozen or so negatives. They would wait and wait for the right moment, when two hockey players collided or a running back headed downfield. Catching peak action took patience and quick thinking.

By the 1960s, photographers were using small, 35-millimeter cameras that allowed them to take 36 shots before changing film. Long telephoto lenses put photogs in the middle of the action. But time continued to work against them. The deadline dash meant that film had to be rushed back to the office, processed quickly and often printed wet.

Now, photographers use digital cameras, which give them the chance to take hundreds of photos before reloading and the chance to transmit photos directly back to the office. A late-inning home run can be placed into the sports section in a matter of seconds. But the process of getting the picture that tells the story remains the same.

The old negatives and prints have been carefully filed away. They are the accumulation of decades of work. Stored upright in cardboard boxes, metal files or on movable shelves, the negatives and prints wait for the day when they will be pulled out and laid carefully on a scanner to be cast into tiny pixels, arranged once again for a new generation of fans.

That time is now.

THE 1942 CHICAGO SUN PHOTO STAFF. BOTTOM ROW FROM LEFT: TONY BIANCO, JOHN MENDICINO, AL MOSSE, CHARLES GEKLER, LEONARD BASS, RALPH FROST AND CLYDE HODGES. TOP ROW FROM LEFT: GLEN MALME, CARMEN REPORTO, RALPH WALTERS, ALDIS DARRE, AL KOLIN, HAROLD NORMAN, MARJORIE PARSONS, FELIX KUBIK, LOUISE CLARKE, SID MAUTNER, DORIS WALLACE, AL VICKER, DAVE MANN, BILL STURM, WILLIAM BENDER, JOHN PAGORIA, BILL KNEFEL AND JOE KORDICK.

"I REMEMBER THE NIGHT JOE LOUIS BEAT JAMES J. BRADDOCK TO WIN THE HEAVYWEIGHT CROWN IN 1937. MY MEMORIES ARE DISTINCT, BUT THE NIGHT WAS CONFUSING.

"I WAS NOT MUCH OF A BOXING FAN AT THE TIME. I HAD GONE TO A COUPLE OF SMALL FIGHTS, BUT SEEING A HEAVYWEIGHT CHAMPIONSHIP FIGHT WAS A WHOLE DIFFERENT EXPERIENCE. I WAS GIVEN TWO TICKETS BY A CLIENT, JULIAN BLACK, WHO SERVED AS JOE'S BUSINESS ADVISER AND MANAGER. I WENT WITH MY FATHER. WE SAT IN THE TENTH ROW RINGSIDE.

"MY MOST VIVID MEMORY OF THE FIGHT WAS TOBACCO SMOKE. COMISKEY PARK SMELLED LIKE TOBACCO. IT SEEMED LIKE EVERYBODY WAS SMOKING.

"I KNEW JOE ONLY PERFUNCTORILY AT THE TIME. JOE WAS NOT A GREAT CONVERSATIONALIST, AND WHEN WE FIRST MET, WE ONLY TALKED ABOUT PEOPLE WE BOTH KNEW IN DETROIT.

"I WAS, OF COURSE, ROOTING FOR JOE BECAUSE I KNEW HIM AND BECAUSE I WAS FRIENDS WITH HIS FRIENDS. ALMOST ALL AFRICAN AMERICANS WERE ROOTING FOR JOE, ALTHOUGH WE HAD A LOT OF RESPECT FOR BRADDOCK.

"IN THE FIRST ROUND, JOE WAS OPEN TO PUNCHES. HE WAS KNOCKED DOWN BY BRADDOCK, BUT JOE CAME BACK. BRADDOCK WAS TOUGH, TAKING PUNCH AFTER PUNCH, BUT JOE CAME ON, ROUND AFTER ROUND, AND KEPT AT THE CHAMPION.

"IT WAS MOST EXCITING TO BE AT THE BOUT, BUT IN A PERVERSE WAY. THE CROWDS, THE SMELL, THE FEELINGS. ALL THIS WAS NEW TO ME, AND I REMEMBER MY EMOTIONS GOT THE BETTER OF ME. THAT WAS A UNIQUE EXPERIENCE; I SELDOM GOT CAUGHT UP IN EVENTS. I THINK WE ALL GOT CAUGHT UP IN THE FIGHT.

"I REMEMBER WALKING TO OUR HOUSE ON THE SOUTH SIDE AFTER THE FIGHT. OUR HOUSE WAS AT 45TH STREET AND MICHIGAN AVENUE, SO WE DIDN'T HAVE A LONG WAY TO GO FROM COMISKEY PARK. I RECALL THAT THE WHOLE SOUTH SIDE ERUPTED. ALL THE RADIOS WERE BLASTING NEWS OF THE FIGHT, AND THERE WAS BEDLAM AND CELEBRATION EVERYWHERE. IT WAS CONFUSING, JUST A MELANGE.

"JOE LOUIS LATER BECAME A CLIENT OF MINE. BEFORE THAT, I HELPED OVERSEE JOE'S STATUS DURING WORLD WAR II, WHILE I WAS WORKING FOR THE SECRETARY OF WAR. I CONSIDERED MYSELF A CLOSE FRIEND OF JOE AFTER THE WAR. WE NEVER TALKED ABOUT THE BRADDOCK FIGHT, OR ABOUT ANY FIGHT. HE SELDOM TALKED MUCH ABOUT BOXING AT ALL. IN FACT, WHEN HE CAME HOME FROM A BOUT, HE WOULD ALWAYS SAY TO HIS WIFE, 'LOOK MARVA, ANOTHER LUCKY FIGHT.' THAT WAS JOE."

—TRUMAN K. GIBSON JR., FORMER PRESIDENT OF THE ILLINOIS BOXING CLUB

PHOTOS FROM LEFT: BABE RUTH, ON THE BOSTON BRAVES; CUBS PITCHER DIZZY DEAN, AND BOXER JOE LOUIS WITH WIFE MARVA.

THE THIRTIES

Pre-race checkup. June 11, 1931
Runners prepare at Soldier Field for the four-mile Daily News Road Race. Each of the 250 runners who reported for numbers was examined by Dr. William Rothman and another physician before being allowed to race. Only three failed the tests.

FIELD DAY. JUNE 11, 1931
RACERS PASS THE FIELD MUSEUM AT THE START OF THE DAILY NEWS ROAD RACE. THEY HEADED DOWN
SOUTH SHORE DRIVE'S INNER DRIVE TO 31ST STREET BEFORE RETURNING TO THE START-FINISH LINE.
BERNARD FRAZIER WON THE RACE IN A TIME OF 21 MINUTES AND 31 SECONDS.

YACHTS OF FUN. AUGUST 28, 1939
TENS OF THOUSANDS OF FANS JAM NAVY PIER TO WATCH THE DAILY NEWS REGATTA. THE ANNUAL EVENT,
WHICH RAN FROM THE 1920S TO THE '40S, WAS THE CLIMAX OF THE LAKE MICHIGAN RACING SEASON.

KING OF THE SOLDIER FIELD MOUNTAIN. FEBRUARY 13, 1938
JORGEN JOHANSEN, OF ROCKFORD, ILLINOIS, LIFTS-OFF IN A SKI JUMP MEET AT SOLDIER FIELD. FANS WATCHED ABOUT 120 JUMPERS COMPETE IN THE THIRD-ANNUAL EVENT, CALLED THE CENTRAL UNITED STATES SKI ASSOCIATION CHAMPIONSHIPS. AN 18-STORY SKI SLIDE—BUILT FOR A $21,000—WAS CONSTRUCTED OF SCAFFOLDING AND COVERED BY SNOW IMPORTED FROM ESCANABA, MICHIGAN.

HERE COME THE CHAMPIONS.
THE 1937-38 CHICAGO BLACKHAWKS WIN THE STANLEY CUP — THE TEAM'S SECOND NATIONAL HOCKEY
LEAGUE CHAMPIONSHIP AND LAST UNTIL 1961. THE 1938 TEAM BARELY MADE THE PLAYOFFS, FINISHING
THE SEASON WITH 14 WINS, 25 LOSSES AND 9 TIES, BUT THEY BEAT THREE TEAMS TO WIN THE CUP. THE
BLACKHAWKS HAD EIGHT AMERICAN-BORN PLAYERS, THE MOST OF ANY CHAMPIONSHIP TEAM.

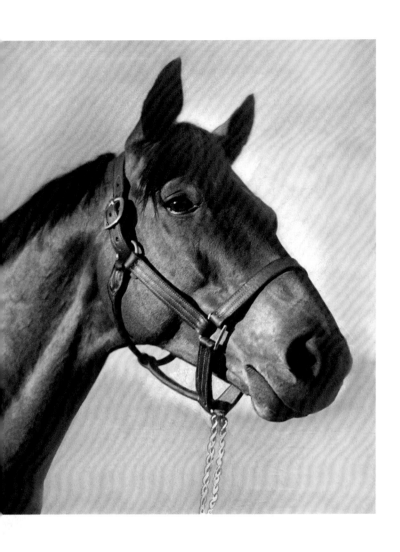

PEOPLE'S CHOICE.
SEABISCUIT LOOKS READY FOR THE $100,000 MEMORIAL DAY MATCH RACE AGAINST WAR ADMIRAL AT BELMONT PARK RACETRACK IN NEW YORK. HE WASN'T. SEABISCUIT'S TRAINER, TOM SMITH, CANCELED THE RACE BECAUSE HIS HORSE WAS SORE. THE THOROUGHBRED RETURNED TO ACTION THE NEXT MONTH AT ARLINGTON PARK. HE LATER DID BEAT WAR ADMIRAL AT PIMLICO RACECOURSE IN BALTIMORE.

PADDOCK PARADE.
HORSES ARE PUT ON DISPLAY AT THE ARLINGTON PARK PADDOCK IN SUBURBAN ARLINGTON HEIGHTS IN 1936. THE TRACK HAS BEEN AN INNOVATOR SINCE IT OPENED IN 1927. DURING THE 1930S, THE PARK INSTALLED THE FIRST ELECTRIC TOTALISATOR, OR TOTE BOARD, THAT CALCULATED PAYOFF ODDS, AND INSTALLED CHICAGO'S FIRST PHOTO-FINISH CAMERA.

SKY RACERS.
AIRPLANE RACING AND EXHIBITIONS WERE POPULAR SPORTS DURING THE EARLY YEARS OF AVIATION, START-
ING WITH THE NATIONAL AIR RACES IN 1920. HERE, SPECTATORS STRAIN TO SEE AN AVIATION SHOW ABOVE
CHICAGO IN 1931. (PHOTO BY ALDEN BROWN.) TOP RIGHT: U.S. ARMY PURSUIT AND COMBAT PLANES FLY
ABOVE CURTISS-REYNOLDS AIRPORT ON THE GLENVIEW NAVAL AIR BASE. THE MILITARY FLIERS TOOK
PART IN THE 1930 NATIONAL AIR RACES, ALONG WITH HUNDREDS OF CIVILIAN PILOTS. RIGHT: AMELIA
EARHART, THE PRIDE OF HYDE PARK HIGH SCHOOL, WAS AN AIR RACER BEFORE HER WORLD EXPEDITIONS.
SHE PARTICIPATED IN MANY AIR DERBIES AND CROSS-COUNTRY RACES BEFORE HER DEATH IN 1937.

MARATHONS OF THE DEPRESSION.
DANCERS COMPETE IN A MARATHON AT THE PERSHING BALLROOM, COTTAGE GROVE AVENUE AT 64TH STREET, ON OC-
TOBER 4, 1930. CITY OFFICIALS ATTEMPTED TO BAN MARATHONS BECAUSE THE EVENTS LASTED UP TO FOUR MONTHS.
LEFT: CHARLEY WINTER (LEFT) AND FRED SPENCER PREPARE A BIKE FOR A SIX-DAY BICYCLE RACE AT CHICAGO
STADIUM. THE ENDURANCE RACES WERE ESPECIALLY POPULAR AMONG WOMEN. WROTE JACK RYAN, IN THE CHICAGO
DAILY NEWS, "THE BIKERS GO 'ROUND 'N' 'ROUND AND FEMININE HEARTS GO FLIPPITY-FLOP. CUPID IS TAKING A
ONE-WAY RIDE ON EVERY SET OF HANDLE BARS."

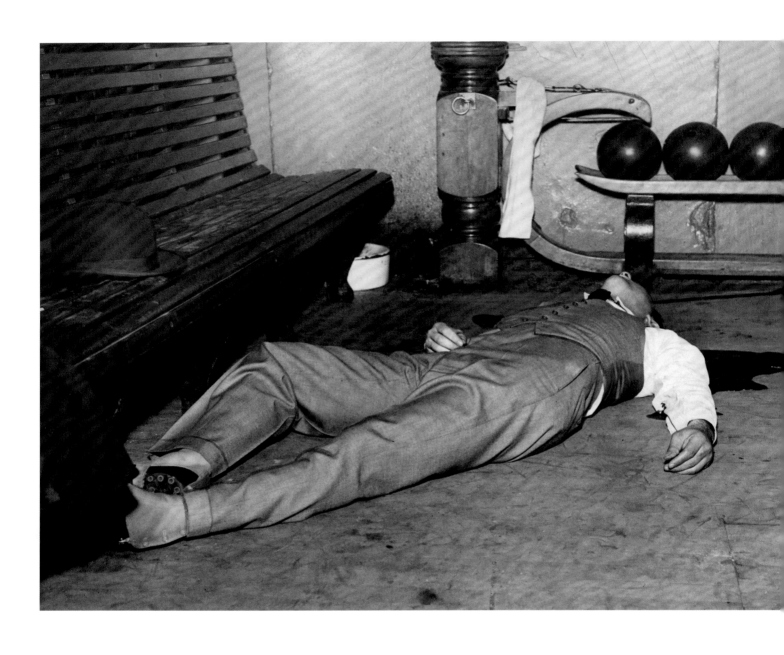

ST. VALENTINE'S NIGHT MASSACRE. FEBRUARY 15, 1936
"MACHINE GUN" JACK MCGURN IS SHOT TO DEATH AT THE AVENUE RECREATION BOWLING ALLEY, 805 NORTH MILWAU-
KEE AVENUE, SEVEN YEARS AFTER THE ST. VALENTINE'S DAY MASSACRE. MCGURN, WHO WAS AL CAPONE'S TRIGGER
MAN, WAS AN EXPERT GOLFER WHO PLAYED ONCE IN THE WESTERN OPEN—UNTIL BEING OUTED AS A GANGSTER. HE WAS
WAITING FOR HIS TURN TO BOWL WHEN HE WAS GUNNED DOWN A FEW MINUTES AFTER MIDNIGHT.

SLIDE, TWILA, SLIDE. JULY 13, 1938
TWILA SHIVLEY DEMONSTRATES THE ART OF SLIDING. SHE WAS ON A SOFTBALL TEAM SPONSORED BY THE HYDROX
BEVERAGE AND ICE CREAM COMPANY. THE ORIGINAL CAPTION READS THAT SHIVLEY "SHOWS PLENTY OF PEPPER
IN SLIDING, AND GETS A CHANCE TO BRING OUT A BIT MORE OF THE AMAZON SATURDAY, SUNDAY AND MONDAY
AGAINST WINNIPEG AT SHEWBRIDGE FIELD."

BABY BEARS.
MEMBERS OF THE 1932 CHICAGO BEARS CHAMPIONSHIP TEAM LINE UP ON THE PRACTICE FIELD. FROM LEFT ARE GUARD PAUL ENGEBRETSEN, END BILL HEWITT, QUARTERBACK ALBERT MOORE AND CENTER CHARLES "OOKIE" MILLER. RIGHT: BRONKO NAGURSKI HOLDS HIS SON, BRONKO JR., IN 1939. NAGURSKI LED THE BEARS TO CHAMPIONSHIPS IN 1932 AND 1933. HE RETIRED IN 1938, WHEN HE COULDN'T GET A $6,500 RAISE, BUT RETURNED TO LEAD THE BEARS TO THE NATIONAL FOOTBALL LEAGUE CHAMPIONSHIP IN 1943.

OBSTRUCTED VIEWS.
A CROWD OF 51,000 WATCH THE WHITE SOX PLAY THE NEW YORK YANKEES ON JULY 23, 1939. TOP RIGHT: THE ST. LOUIS BROWNS TAKE ON THE SOX ON APRIL 14, 1932. RIGHT: SOX PLAYER-MANAGER JIMMY DYKES GIVES LAST-MINUTE INSTRUCTIONS BEFORE TAKING THE FIELD ON MAY 18, 1934. FROM LEFT ARE FRENCHY UHALT, BOB BOKEN, MUDDY RUEL, ZEKE BONURA, DYKES AND GEORGE EARNSHAW. THE SOX FINISHED IN LAST PLACE, LOSING 99 GAMES.

FOOLING AROUND.
SLUGGER AL SIMMONS POSES WITH HIS 19-YEAR-OLD BRIDE, DORES READER, OF ROGERS PARK, ON THEIR HONEY-
MOON IN LAUDERDALE, WISCONSIN, ON AUGUST 10, 1934. SIMMONS' AVERAGE DROPPED 77 PERCENTAGE POINTS THE
FOLLOWING YEAR. "TEAMMATES DECLARED THAT AL PROMPTLY BECAME TOO ROMANTICALLY MINDED TO PLAY SERIOUS
BASEBALL," A REPORTER WROTE. RIGHT: WHITE SOX MANAGER JIMMY DYKES TAKES PRECAUTION ON JULY 6, 1939,
AFTER HE WAS SUSPENDED FOR ARGUING WITH AN UMPIRE.

TEN-SHUN, TEN-SHUN PLEASE.
THE CUBS' PAT PIEPER GATHERS STRAW HATS SHOWERED BY FANS ON SEPTEMBER 1, 1932. PIEPER ANNOUNCED FOR THE TEAM FOR 59 YEARS, STARTING EACH GAME: "GET YOUR PENCILS AND SCORECARDS READY FOR THE CORRECT LINEUP." RIGHT: CUBS PITCHER GUY BUSH IS CALLED OUT AT THE PLATE AFTER BEING TAGGED BY NEW YORK GIANTS CATCHER SHANTY HOGAN ON JULY 15, 1931. THIS WAS BEFORE THE WRIGLEY FIELD BLEACHERS WERE BUILT.

STILL IN THE GLOAMIN'. OCTOBER 3, 1938
CUBS CATCHER GABBY HARTNETT LEADS THE TEAM'S
VICTORY PARADE DOWN LASALLE STREET AFTER THE
CUBS WON THE PENNANT. HARTNETT'S FAMOUS "HOM-
ER IN THE GLOAMIN'" SET UP THE PENNANT FOR THE
CUBS. HARTNETT TOOK OVER AS MANAGER OF THE
CUBS IN LATE JULY AND WILLED THE TEAM FROM
FOURTH PLACE TO FIRST. THE PARADE STARTED AT
WRIGLEY FIELD AND HEADED DOWNTOWN.

HALL-OF-FAME MATCHUP. OCTOBER 6, 1938
RIGHT: THE CUBS' DIZZY DEAN STRIKES OUT YAN-
KEES' JOE DIMAGGIO IN THE SEVENTH INNING OF
GAME 2 OF THE WORLD SERIES. TWO INNINGS LATER,
DIMAGGIO HOMERED OFF DEAN. "ONE MOMENT DIZZY
DEAN WAS WINNING THE GREATEST BATTLE OF HIS CA-
REER, THE NEXT HE WAS DEFEATED, 6 TO 3," WROTE
DAILY TIMES SPORTS EDITOR MARVIN MCCARTHY.
THE YANKS SWEPT THE SERIES.

EARLY GLIMPSE OF GREATNESS.
JESSE OWENS, A SENIOR AT CLEVELAND EAST TECHNICAL HIGH SCHOOL, ARRIVES AT THE INTERSCHOLASTIC CHAMPIONSHIPS AT SOLDIER FIELD IN AUGUST 1932. OWENS TIED THE WORLD RECORD IN THE 100-YARD DASH WITH A TIME OF 9.4 SECONDS AND SET SEVERAL HIGH SCHOOL RECORDS. FOUR YEARS LATER, HE DOMINATED THE SUMMER OLYMPIC GAMES IN BERLIN BY WINNING FOUR GOLD MEDALS.

ME TARZAN; YOU JANES.
MOVIE STAR JOHNNY WEISSMULLER TAKES A CHEERFUL SHOVE FROM ARMIDA AND MARY BRIAN AS THEY FROLIC ALONG LAKE MICHIGAN IN 1932. WEISSMULLER LEARNED TO SWIM AT FULLERTON AVENUE BEACH. HE WON FIVE GOLD MEDALS DURING THE 1924 AND 1928 OLYMPIC GAMES AND HELD EVERY FREESTYLE RECORD IN THE WORLD FROM THE 100-YARD DASH TO HALF-MILE SWIM. HE WENT ON TO HOLLYWOOD TO STAR IN A DOZEN TARZAN MOVIES.

A GAME FOR CITY AND COUNTRY.
ABOVE: CHARLES HAMILTON PUTTS AT THE MEDINAH COUNTRY CLUB IN SUBURBAN MEDINAH. THE $3 MILLION MOORISH MARVEL WAS BUILT BY THE CHICAGO SHRINERS IN THE 1920S TO BE THE WORLD'S MOST ELABORATE, LARGEST COUNTRY CLUB. (PHOTO BY ANDREW T. MILLER.) TOP RIGHT: AN EIGHTSOME. RIGHT: CONTENDERS IN THE FINALS OF A PUTTING CHAMPIONSHIP AT MID-CITY GOLF LINKS AT ADDISON AND WESTERN AVENUES ON AUGUST 16, 1930. THEY INCLUDED, FROM LEFT: MRS. MARY BEATTY, MRS. J.H. TWITCHELL, ROSE JOHNSON, MRS. FRANCES McDYER AND MRS. AL DEMAREE. THE COURSE WAS REPLACED BY LANE TECHNICAL HIGH SCHOOL.

A NEW CHAMPION. JUNE 22, 1937
JOE LOUIS KNOCKS OUT HEAVYWEIGHT CHAM-
PION JAMES J. BRADDOCK, KNOWN AS "THE
CINDERELLA MAN," IN THE EIGHTH ROUND OF
THE HEAVYWEIGHT CHAMPIONSHIP AT COMIS-
KEY PARK. BRADDOCK KNOCKED LOUIS DOWN
IN THE FIRST ROUND OF THE FIGHT, BUT THE
23-YEAR-OLD LOUIS BATTLED BACK. "IT SEEMS
LIKE A DREAM AND I PINCH MYSELF TO REALIZE
THAT I'M NOW HEAVYWEIGHT CHAMPION OF THE
WORLD," LOUIS WROTE IN THE DAILY TIMES
THE NEXT MORNING. LOUIS HELD THE HEAVY-
WEIGHT CHAMPIONSHIP UNTIL HE RETIRED FOR
THE FIRST TIME IN 1949.

"I FIRST CAME TO THE CHICAGO CUBS AT THE TAIL END OF THE 1943 SEASON FOR ABOUT 13 GAMES. OF COURSE, I HAD NEVER BEEN TO CHICAGO BEFORE AND HAD NEVER SEEN WRIGLEY FIELD. THAT WAS QUITE A THRILL FOR ME, AND I'LL NEVER FORGET MY FIRST TIME AT BAT. I THINK THAT I HAD AN EXTRA BASE HIT AND DROVE IN A COUPLE OF RUNS, AND THEN I GOT ANOTHER HIT AND DROVE IN TWO MORE RUNS. IT WAS A GOOD FEELING TO HAVE THAT SUCCESS RIGHT AWAY.

"I WILL NEVER FORGET THE FEELING OF FIRST SEEING WRIGLEY FIELD. I'LL NEVER FORGET WALKING INTO THE CUBS CLUBHOUSE FOR THE FIRST TIME. WHEN I OPENED THE DOOR, THE FIRST GUY I MET WAS STAN HACK, THE CUBS' THIRD BASEMAN. I RECOGNIZED HIM, AND I'LL NEVER FORGET WHAT HE SAID. 'ANDY PAFKO, WELCOME TO THE BIG LEAGUES, WELCOME TO CHICAGO.' THAT WAS THE GREATEST MOMENT OF MY LIFE.

"I PLAYED OUTFIELD, PRIMARILY IN CENTER, BUT I ALSO PLAYED RIGHT AND LEFT. WHEN STAN HACK RETIRED, THEY MOVED ME TO THIRD BASE. TO ME, IT WAS JUST A THRILL TO BE IN THE BIG LEAGUES. I THINK THAT THE GREATEST FANS ARE IN CHICAGO. THEY HAVE TO BE. THEY'VE BEEN SO LOYAL ALL THESE YEARS.

"THE YEAR THE CUBS WERE IN THE WORLD SERIES, 1945, WAS A GREAT YEAR FOR ME AND FOR THE TEAM. WE WERE BATTLING THE CARDINALS FOR THE CHAMPIONSHIP, AND I DROVE IN THE WINNING RUN WITH A FLY BALL TO RIGHT FIELD. THAT PUT US INTO THE WORLD SERIES.

"I DIDN'T MOVE TO CHICAGO AT FIRST. I HAD ALWAYS LIVED BACK HOME IN WISCONSIN. AFTER I PLAYED FOR THE CUBS FOR A COUPLE OF YEARS, I MET A GIRL IN CHICAGO THROUGH A MUTUAL FRIEND, AND WE GOT MARRIED. THEN, OF COURSE, I MADE MY HOME IN CHICAGO. WE FIRST LIVED ON THE NORTHWEST SIDE, THEN WE MOVED TO THE KELVYN PARK NEIGHBORHOOD, WHERE WE LIVED FOR 20 YEARS BEFORE MOVING TO MOUNT PROSPECT.

"WHEN I WAS LIVING IN CHICAGO, I USED TO DRIVE TO THE BASEBALL GAMES AT WRIGLEY FIELD. I DROVE MY CAR THE SAME ROUTE EVERY DAY FOR A LONG, LONG TIME. IF I HAD A GOOD GAME, I TOOK THE SAME ROUTE. IF I HAD A BAD GAME, I WOULD CHANGE MY ROUTE TO CHANGE MY LUCK. I WAS KIND OF SUPERSTITIOUS. I DON'T KNOW IF IT HELPED A LOT, BUT I THINK THAT MOST BALLPLAYERS HAVE THEIR OWN PET SUPERSTITIONS.

"PEOPLE SAY TO ME, 'ANDY. DON'T YOU WISH YOU WERE PLAYING TODAY WITH ALL THE BIG SALARIES?' I SAY, 'NO.' PERSONALLY, I HAVE NO REGRETS. I PLAYED IN THE GREATEST ERA OF ALL, IN THE '40S AND '50S AGAINST JOE DIMAGGIO, TED WILLIAMS, BOB FELLER, STAN MUSIAL, AND JACKIE ROBINSON. YOU CAN'T REPLACE THOSE GUYS."

—ANDY PAFKO, FORMER CHICAGO CUBS OUTFIELDER

CLOCKWISE FROM TOP LEFT: NORTHWESTERN UNIVERSITY FOOTBALL PRACTICE PHOTO BY AL MOSSE, CUBS OUTFIELDER ANDY PAFKO PHOTO BY MICKEY RITO, AND WHITE SOX PLAYERS DON KOLLOWAY (FROM LEFT), FRANK KALIN AND SKEETER WEBB PHOTO BY BILL STURM.

THE FORTIES

RACE ACROSS THE LAKE.
PHOTO BY DAVE MANN, JUNE 18, 1944
SIXTY-SIX YACHTS LEAVE CHICAGO FOR A 37-MILE RACE TO MICHIGAN CITY, INDIANA. THE ANNUAL RACE, SPONSORED BY THE COLUMBIA YACHT CLUB, WAS STARTED IN 1892, THE YEAR THE CLUB WAS FOUNDED. IT WAS THE OLDEST FRESHWATER YACHT RACE IN THE WORLD.

THERE GOES THE CHAMP. SEPTEMBER 10, 1942
JOE LOUIS WAVES TO A CROWD AS HE PASSES THROUGH CHICAGO ON HIS WAY TO A NEW TRAINING CAMP. LOUIS
DEFENDED HIS HEAVYWEIGHT TITLE 21 TIMES BEFORE ENLISTING IN THE ARMY AS A PRIVATE. HE FOUGHT
ABOUT 100 EXHIBITION MATCHES BEFORE AN ESTIMATED 2 MILLION SERVICEMEN AS A GI. HE ALSO DONATED
HIS SHARE FROM TWO CHAMPIONSHIP FIGHTS TO MILITARY FUNDS. "MIGHT BE A LOT WRONG WITH AMERICA,
BUT NOTHING HITLER CAN FIX," HE SAID.

THE LONG PATH TO WAR. PHOTO BY MEL LARSON, APRIL 24, 1943
MARINE SERGEANT BARNEY ROSS (SECOND FROM RIGHT) AND SAILOR SHELBY PITTS SALUTE THE COLORS AT
A DOWNTOWN WAR BONDS PARADE. ROSS, WHO GREW UP IN CHICAGO, WON THE WORLD LIGHTWEIGHT, JUNIOR
WELTERWEIGHT AND WELTERWEIGHT CHAMPIONSHIPS DURING THE 1930S. HE RECEIVED A SILVER STAR FOR
BRAVERY DURING WORLD WAR II, BUT SUFFERED SHELL SHOCK AND WAS WOUNDED AT GUADALCANAL. ROSS BE-
CAME ADDICTED TO MORPHINE GIVEN TO HIM DURING HIS HOSPITAL STAY, BUT HE RECOVERED AFTER THE WAR.

BACK IN ACTION.
HAROLD E. "RED" GRANGE, ONE OF THE ALL-TIME GREAT RUNNING BACKS, TEACHES FOOTBALL ON SEPTEMBER 29, 1948. GRANGE STARRED FOR THE UNIVERSITY OF ILLINOIS IN THE EARLY 1920S AND FOR THE BEARS IN 1925 AND FROM 1929 TO 1935. (PHOTO BY BILL STURM.) TOP RIGHT: JIM THORPE, 61, THE GREATEST ALL-AROUND ATHLETE OF THE CENTURY, KEEPS UP WITH KIDS IN 1948. RIGHT: BABE RUTH SIGNS AN AUTOGRAPH DURING A STOP IN CHICAGO. (PHOTO BY CHARLES GEKLER.)

REACHING FOR THE STARS.
FULLBACK DOC BLANCHARD (LEFT), FROM WEST POINT, AND HALFBACK CHARLEY TRIPPI, FROM THE UNIVERSITY OF
GEORGIA, TAKE A BREAK AT THE COLLEGE ALL-STARS' PRACTICE ON AUGUST 20, 1947. THE COLLEGE ALL-STAR GAME,
BETWEEN THE NFL CHAMPIONS AND COLLEGE STARS, WAS A PRESEASON TRADITION AT SOLDIER FIELD FROM 1934 TO
1976. TRIPPI LATER STARRED IN THE CHICAGO CARDINALS' "DREAM BACKFIELD." (PHOTO BY LEONARD BASS.) LEFT:
JOHNNY LATTNER SNARES A PASS IN PRACTICE AT FENWICK HIGH SCHOOL ON SEPTEMBER 30, 1948. LATTNER, ONE OF
THE GREAT CATHOLIC LEAGUE PLAYERS OF ALL TIME, TOOK FENWICK TO TWO PREP BOWL CITY CHAMPIONSHIP GAMES AND
WENT ON TO WIN THE HEISMAN TROPHY AT NOTRE DAME. (PHOTO BY MICKEY RITO.)

BEST OF THE BEARS.
HALL OF FAME QUARTERBACK SID LUCKMAN AND HALL OF FAME CENTER CLYDE "BULLDOG" TURNER DEM-
ONSTRATE THEIR SECRET HIKE ON SEPTEMBER 4, 1943. "WHEN TURNER HANDS THE BALL BACK TO HIM, HE
PASSES IT IN SUCH A WAY THAT THE LACES ALWAYS ARE AGAINST LUCKMAN'S FINGERS, IN PERFECT POSITION
FOR PASSING," EXPLAINED THE TIMES. LEFT: THE BEARS PREPARE DECEMBER 10, 1941, FOR THE NFL WEST-
ERN DIVISION CHAMPIONSHIP GAME AT WRIGLEY FIELD. HERE, BEARS OWNER-COACH GEORGE HALAS (LEFT)
SHOWS GAME PLANS TO YOUNG BUSSEY (FROM LEFT), BOB SNYDER, KEN KAVANAUGH AND DICK PLASMAN. THE
BEARS WON FOUR NFL CHAMPIONSHIPS DURING THE 1940S — IN 1940, 1941, 1943 AND 1946.

ANOTHER LEAGUE OF THEIR OWN. JUNE 26, 1941
WOMEN'S FOOTBALL—CALLED GIRLS' FOOTBALL IN THE AGE—WAS INTRODUCED, BRIEFLY, TO CHICAGO JUST BEFORE THE START OF WORLD WAR II. THE DAILY TIMES RAN A PICTURE STORY THE NIGHT BEFORE THE TEAMS SQUARED OFF AT SPENCER COALS FIELD, BUT THE PAPER NEVER RAN A FOLLOWUP STORY. ABOVE: DOROTHY BROWN, A TACKLE FOR THE BOMBERS, PROUDLY DISPLAYED A BLACK EYE SUFFERED IN PRACTICE. TOP RIGHT: THE ROCKETS AND THE BOMBERS PRACTICE BEFORE THE FIRST GAME. RIGHT: WOMEN POSE AS FEMININE WARRIORS. THEY ARE (FROM LEFT) EDNA RITTER, SOPHIE ARAMIAN AND FRITZIE HECHTMAN.

LINKS TO THE PAST.
BEN HOGAN ON THE GREEN JULY 9, 1944. HOGAN WON THREE CHICAGO OPEN TITLES. FACING PAGE, CLOCKWISE FROM TOP LEFT: AMATEUR STAR CHICK EVANS, WHO SET UP THE EVANS SCHOLARS PROGRAM, SHOOTS FROM THE ROUGH ON AUGUST 13, 1944. (PHOTO BY BILL STURM.) BABE DIDRIKSON ZAHARIAS ON AUGUST 19, 1946. (PHOTO BY CHARLES GECKLER.) BOBBY JONES AT A PRACTICE ROUND ON APRIL 2, 1947, BEFORE THE MASTERS TOURNAMENT IN AUGUSTA, GEORGIA. (PHOTO BY CHARLES GEKLER.) BYRON NELSON AND HIS WIFE, LOUISE, ADMIRE HIS TROPHY AFTER WINNING THE TAM O'SHANTER OPEN IN SUBURBAN NILES ON JULY 27, 1942. (PHOTO BY DAVE MANN.)

GRACE AND GORE ON THE ICE.
FIGURE SKATING CHAMPION SONJA HENIE GLIDES WITH HER PARTNER, MICHAEL KIRBY, AT THE CHICAGO STADIUM ON DECEMBER 26, 1949. HENIE WON 10 CONSECUTIVE WORLD FIGURE SKATING CHAMPIONSHIPS AND GOLD MEDALS AT THREE OLYMPICS. (PHOTO BY LOUIS OKMIN.) LEFT: BLACKHAWKS JOHNNY MARIUCCI THROWS A PUNCH AT DETROIT RED WINGS JACK STEWART IN THE THIRD PERIOD OF A GAME AT THE CHICAGO STADIUM ON DECEMBER 4, 1946. THE PHOTOGRAPHER WROTE: "MAIN EVENT STARTS IN THE PENALTY BOX. IT'S A SHOW STOPPER AS MARIUCCI LETS FLY AND STEWART FLIES BACK AT HIM." (PHOTO BY MICKEY RITO.)

Exhibition season.

Ten-year-old Bobby Berner, of suburban Winnetka, takes pictures of Cubs players in the Wrigley Field dugout during the preseason city series between the Cubs and White Sox on April 16, 1948. (Photo by Al Mosse.) Right: Cubs outfielder Lou Novikoff rattles opponents, and his team, on April 7, 1943. The Mad Russian—actually from Glendale, Arizona—was one of the most highly touted minor leaguers ever to hit the big leagues. But Novikoff had problems in the Friendly Confines; he was afraid of the Wrigley Field ivy. (Photo by Mickey Rito.)

No fooling; Cubs win. October 8, 1945
Cubs manager Charlie Grimm rustles the hair of his third baseman, Stan Hack, after the Cubs beat the Tigers 8-7 to tie the World Series at three games apiece. Hack went 4 for 5 and batted in the winning run on a double in the 12th inning. Left: Before the game, Grimm talked about the Cubs' defeat in Game 5 and correctly predicted victory.

LAST SERIES LINEUP.
PHOTO BY MEL LARSON, OCTOBER 10, 1945
FANS CONGREGATE TO BUY BLEACHER TICKETS FOR THE
DECIDING GAME OF THE 1945 WORLD SERIES. MORE THAN
41,000 SPECTATORS JAMMED WRIGLEY FIELD TO WATCH
THE DETROIT TIGERS BEAT THE CUBS 9-3 AND TAKE THE
SERIES 4 GAMES TO 3.

INSTANT REPLAY.
**PHOTO BY CHARLES GECKLER,
MAY 19, 1947**
PHIL CAVARETTA IS THROWN OUT
ON A CLOSE PLAY AT FIRST BASE AS
BROOKLYN DODGERS PITCHER JOE
HATTEN COVERS THE BAG. JACKIE
ROBINSON, SHOWN IN THE BACK-
GROUND, TOSSED THE BALL. IT
WAS ROBINSON'S FIRST SERIES AT
WRIGLEY FIELD.

JUST VISITING. PHOTOS BY CHARLES GEKLER.
OUTFIELDER DOM DIMAGGIO, JOE'S BROTHER, HEADS OUT TO THE COMISKEY PARK OUTFIELD IN 1946. FACING
PAGE, CLOCKWISE FROM TOP LEFT: JACKIE ROBINSON IN 1947, STAN MUSIAL, TED WILLIAMS AND YOGI BERRA
ON MARCH 13, 1947. GEKLER'S CAPTION, FROM SPRING TRAINING IN ST. PETERSBURG, FLORIDA, READS:
"LAWRENCE BERRA, ROOKIE CATCHER WHO IS BEING TRIED OUT IN RIGHT FIELD."

COMISKEY CAPADES.
WHITE SOX CATCHER RALPH WEIGEL TAGS OUT CLEVELAND INDIANS CATCHER JIM HEGAN WHEN HE TRIED TO
SCORE FROM THIRD ON A FLY TO RIGHT FIELD ON SEPTEMBER 7, 1948. LARRY DOBY (FOREGROUND) DIRECTS
THE PLAY. (PHOTO BY MICKEY RITO.) TOP RIGHT: SOX SHORTSTOP LUKE APPLING CHECKS OUT A CAR PURCHASED
BY APPRECIATIVE SOX FANS ON LUKE APPLING DAY, JUNE 8, 1947. (PHOTO BY CHARLES GEKLER.) RIGHT: SOX
MANAGER JIMMY DYKES SHOWS HIS FOUR ACES ON MAY 11, 1945. THEY ARE (FROM LEFT) PITCHERS ED LOPAT,
JOE HAYNES, THORNTON LEE AND ORVAL GROVE. THEY WON 44 GAMES AMONG THEM. (PHOTO BY AL MOSSE.)

CHEERLEADERS. PHOTOS BY
AL MOSSE, MARCH 22, 1942

THE MIKAN DRILL. 1946.
GEORGE MIKAN, BASKETBALL'S FIRST
DOMINATING BIG MAN, SHOWS WHAT
AN AGILE, NEAR-7-FOOTER CAN DO ON
THE COURT. MIKAN, BORN IN JOLIET,
ILLINOIS, PLAYED FOR DePAUL UNI-
VERSITY AND LED THE CHICAGO AMER-
ICAN GEARS TO THEIR FIRST NATIONAL
BASKETBALL LEAGUE TITLE IN 1947.
HE LATER STARRED IN THE NATIONAL
BASKETBALL ASSOCIATION.

VIVA LA DIFFERENCE. PHOTOS BY CHARLES GEKLER.
"BEVY OF SWIMMING GALS." LEFT: WEIGHTLIFTER. MARCH 9, 1944.

RAGING BULLS. PHOTO BY BILL STURM, DECEMBER 3, 1945
BOXER JAKE LAMOTTA (LEFT) POSES WITH HIS BROTHER, JOEY, AT THE CATHOLIC YOUTH ORGANIZATION GYM. JAKE KNOCKED
OUT CHARLEY PARHAM FOUR DAYS LATER IN CHICAGO. LAMOTTA WON THE WORLD MIDDLEWEIGHT CHAMPIONSHIP IN 1949.
JOEY LAMOTTA WAS HIS MANAGER. RIGHT: EZZARD CHARLES COLLECTS HIMSELF AFTER BEATING JERSEY JOE WALCOTT
AND WINNING THE NATIONAL BOXING ASSOCIATION HEAVYWEIGHT TITLE AT COMISKEY PARK ON JUNE 22, 1949. IT WAS
CHARLES' FIFTH TRY. IN 1950, CHARLES DEFEATED JOE LOUIS, WHO CAME OUT OF RETIREMENT, AND WAS PROCLAIMED THE
WORLD HEAVYWEIGHT CHAMPION.

SOUTH SIDE TOUGHS.
THE CHICAGO CARDINALS DEFEAT THE PHILADELPHIA EAGLES 28-21 IN THE 1947 NFL CHAMPIONSHIP GAME AT COMISKEY PARK. LEFT: THE CARDINALS CELEBRATE AFTER DEFEATING THE COLLEGE ALL-STARS 28-0 AT SOLDIER FIELD ON AUGUST 20, 1948, BEFORE 101,220 FANS. THE 1948 TEAM WENT ON TO COMPILE AN 11-1 SEASON RECORD, BUT IT LOST TO THE EAGLES IN THE NFL CHAMPIONSHIP GAME. ALL-PRO TACKLE STAN MAULDIN (77) DIED OF A HEART ATTACK IN THE CARDINALS' DRESSING ROOM AFTER THE TEAM'S FIRST REGULAR SEASON GAME THE FOLLOWING MONTH.

THE GOOD KID COMES HOME. PHOTO BY BILL STURM, OCTOBER 28, 1948

LOU BOUDREAU GREETS CROWDS AS HE IS PARADED DOWN THE STREETS OF HOMETOWN HARVEY, ILLINOIS, WITH GOVERNOR DWIGHT GREEN. BOUDREAU MANAGED AND PLAYED SHORTSTOP FOR THE CLEVELAND INDI-ANS, WHO WON THE WORLD SERIES THAT YEAR. IN HIGH SCHOOL, HE LED THE THORNTON FLYING CLOUDS BASKETBALL TEAM TO THE STATE CHAMPIONSHIP IN 1933 AND SECOND-PLACE FINISHES IN 1934 AND 1935. HE RETURNED TO SERVE ON THE THORNTON TOWNSHIP HIGH SCHOOL BOARD FOR MANY YEARS.

BACK TO STEELTOWN. PHOTO BY BORRIE KANTER, JUNE 13, 1948
TWO-TIME WORLD MIDDLEWEIGHT BOXING CHAMPION TONY ZALE RETURNS TO HIS HOMETOWN IN GARY, INDIANA, FOR A VICTORY CELEBRATION. KNOWN AS "THE MAN OF STEEL," ZALE WORKED IN GARY'S STEEL MILLS BEFORE TURNING PRO IN 1934. HE IS BEST KNOWN FOR THREE BRUTAL BOUTS AGAINST ROCKY GRAZIANO AFTER WORLD WAR II. ZALE WON TWO OF THE FIGHTS BY KNOCKOUTS.

KEEPER OF THE KEYS.
AL MELGARD DEMONSTRATES ONE OF THE WORLD'S LARGEST PIPE ORGANS AT CHICAGO STADIUM IN 1946.
POLITICAL LORE CREDITS MELGARD WITH PLAYING "HAPPY DAYS ARE HERE AGAIN" AT THE 1932 DEMOCRATIC
NATIONAL CONVENTION AT THE STADIUM. IT BECAME THE THEME SONG FOR THE PARTY. FOR BLACKHAWKS
GAMES, HE WAS KNOWN TO PLAY "THREE BLIND MICE" WHENEVER HE FELT THE REFEREES MADE A BAD CALL.

HIGH STICKING.
JOHNNY GOTTSELIG SHOWS THE NEW TIMEPIECE AT CHICAGO STADIUM IN 1943. GOTTSELIG, A DEFENSEMAN WHO PLAYED ALMOST 600 GAMES FOR THE BLACKHAWKS, WAS A MEMBER OF THE HAWKS' STANLEY CUP TEAMS IN 1934 AND 1938. HE MANAGED THE RACINE BELLES TO THE FIRST CHAMPIONSHIP OF THE ALL-AMERICAN GIRLS PROFESSIONAL BASEBALL LEAGUE AND RETURNED TO COACH THE HAWKS FOR THREE YEARS.

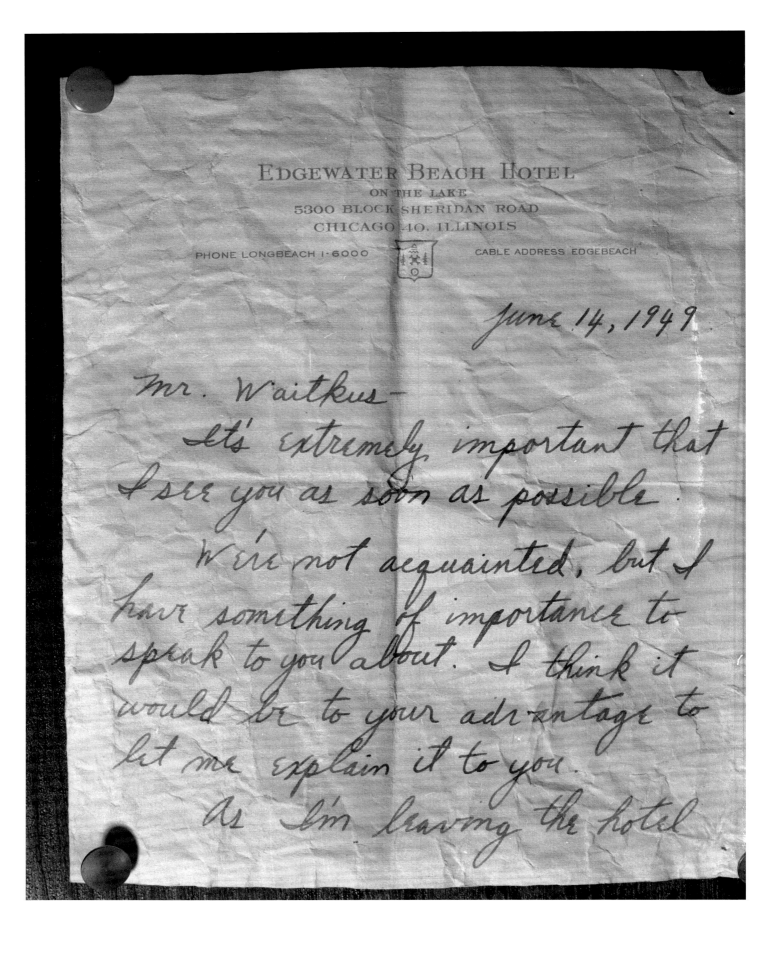

EDGEWATER BEACH HOTEL
ON THE LAKE
5300 BLOCK SHERIDAN ROAD
CHICAGO 40, ILLINOIS

PHONE LONGBEACH 1·6000   CABLE ADDRESS EDGEBEACH

June 14, 1949

Mr. Waitkus—

It's extremely important that I see you as soon as possible.

We're not acquainted, but I have something of importance to speak to you about. I think it would be to your advantage to let me explain it to you.

As I'm leaving the hotel

BRIEFLY NOTED. JUNE 15, 1949
PHILLIES FIRST BASEMAN EDDIE WAITKUS IS RUSHED TO ILLINOIS MASONIC HOSPITAL AFTER BEING CRITICALLY WOUND-
ED AT THE EDGEWATER BEACH HOTEL. LEFT: RUTH ANN STEINHAGEN, A 19-YEAR-OLD FAN WHO HAD A CRUSH ON HIM,
INVITED WAITKUS TO HER HOTEL ROOM AND SHOT HIM WITH A .22-CALIBER RIFLE. SHE WAS DECLARED INSANE BY A JURY
AND COMMITTED TO THE KANKAKEE STATE HOSPITAL. THREE YEARS LATER, SHE WAS RELEASED. WAITKUS RETURNED TO
BASEBALL IN 1950, BUT WAS NEVER THE SAME. THE SHOOTING SERVED AS THE BASIS FOR "THE NATURAL."

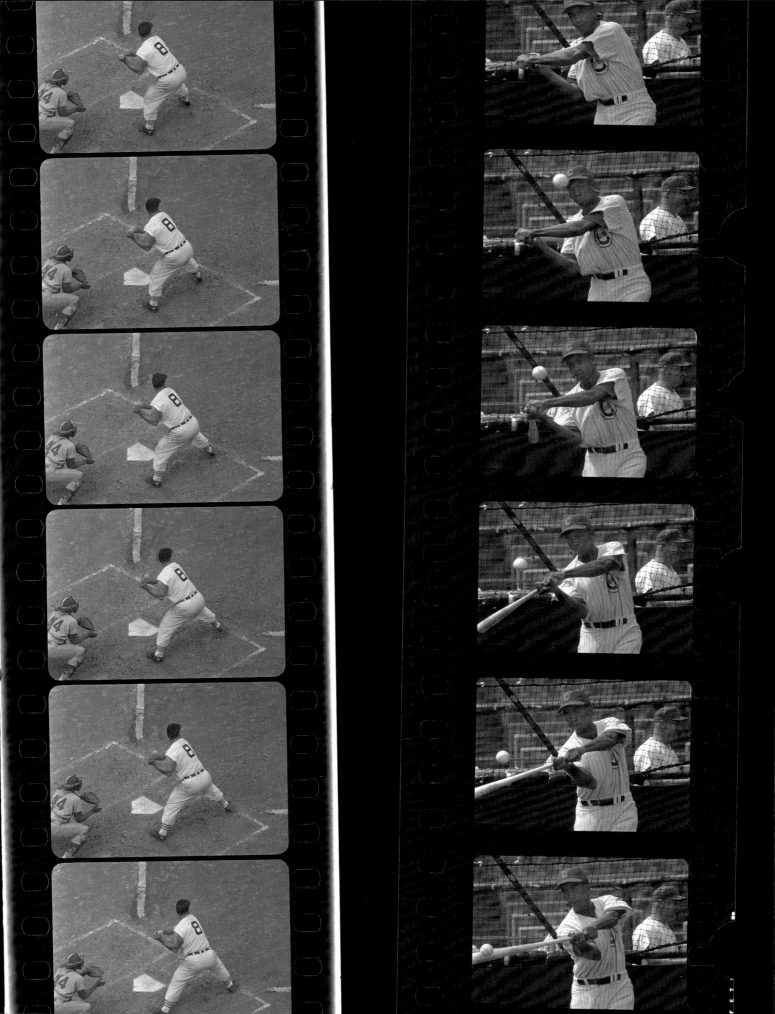

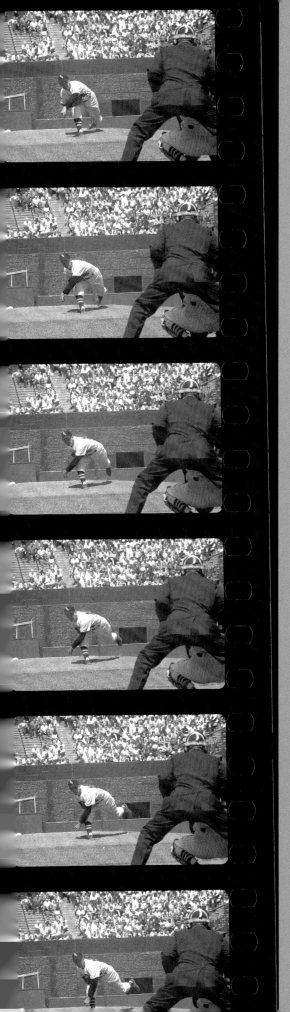

"MY FIRST REACTION TO COMISKEY PARK, WHEN I FIRST CAME THERE WHILE WITH THE DETROIT TIGERS, WAS THE STRONG AROMA FROM THE STOCKYARDS. IT HADN'T REALLY CHANGED WHEN I STARTED PITCHING FOR THE WHITE SOX IN 1949, AND THAT WAS VERY, VERY ROUGH, ESPECIALLY DURING OUR NIGHT GAMES, BUT IT WAS JUST ONE OF THOSE THINGS.

"WHEN THE WIND WAS BLOWING FROM THE SOUTHWEST INTO THE BALLPARK, COMISKEY PARK WASN'T THE MOST PLEASANT PLACE TO BE. THOSE STOCKYARDS HAD QUITE AN AROMA, I'LL TELL YOU THAT.

"WHEN I FIRST GOT TO THE SOX, THEY HAD EXPERIENCED A STRING OF LOSING SEASONS, AND THE FANS WEREN'T COMING TO THE PARK. THE SOX WERE 51-101 IN 1948, BUT AFTER I JOINED THE CLUB, FRANK LANE, THE GENERAL MANAGER, BEGAN MAKING A LOT OF TRADES TO IMPROVE THE TEAM. SO BY 1951, WE HAD THE GO-GO SOX. WE HAD NELLIE FOX AND MINNIE MINOSO AND A PRETTY GOOD BALLCLUB. I THINK THAT BY JULY 4, 1951, WE WERE IN FIRST PLACE. WHAT REALLY GOT US GOING WAS OUR SPEED.

"AS FOR PITCHING IN COMISKEY PARK, WHEN I FIRST GOT THERE, IT WAS A GREAT PARK TO PITCH IN BECAUSE THE DIMENSIONS WERE VERY DEEP. CENTER FIELD WAS 440 FEET FROM HOME PLATE, AND THE WIND SEEMED TO BE BLOWING IN ALL THE TIME. OVER A PERIOD OF YEARS, THE SOX BROUGHT IN THE FENCES AND BUILT A FENCE TO MAKE CENTER FIELD 400 FEET FROM HOME PLATE. THEN, THE WINDS STARTED CHANGING DIRECTIONS. INSTEAD OF BLOWING IN, THEY BEGAN BLOWING OUT. WHAT WAS ONCE A PITCHER'S BALLPARK BECAME A HITTER'S PARK.

"COMISKEY WAS A BEAUTIFUL PARK, AND THE FANS WERE FANTASTIC. THEY WERE ALWAYS BEHIND OUR TEAM, HOLLERING, 'GO, GO, GO.' THEY WOULD STAND ON THE STAIRWAY THAT LED UP TO THE CLUBHOUSE TO GREET US. AND THEY WOULD LINE UP AROUND THE PARKING LOT LOOKING FOR AN AUTOGRAPH OR FOR US TO TAKE A PICTURE WITH THEM. THEY WERE VERY FRIENDLY. WE MUST HAVE HAD ABOUT 10 FAN CLUBS FOR THE PLAYERS, MADE UP OF GIRLS AND BOYS WHO WOULD PULL FOR THEIR FAVORITE PLAYER AND MAKE SIGNS.

"MAYOR RICHARD J. DALEY WAS A GREAT SOX FAN. HE WOULD BRING HIS SONS OUT TO THE BALLGAME QUITE OFTEN AND SIT RIGHT BY THE THIRD-BASE DUGOUT. THE CITY ITSELF BECAME VERY PRO-WHITE SOX IN THE '50s. WE EVEN HAD A PARADE WHEN WE WON 14 GAMES IN A ROW.

"WE USED TO HAVE BIG WEEKEND SERIES WITH THE YANKEES, THE INDIANS AND THE RED SOX. THOSE GAMES PROVIDED MOST OF OUR TOTAL SEASON ATTENDANCE. WE WOULD DRAW FROM 50,000 TO 55,000 FANS TO THOSE GAMES, PARTLY BECAUSE NIGHT GAMES WEREN'T TELEVISED. IT WAS JUST A VERY GOOD TIME FOR THE PLAYERS, FOR THE FANS, AND FOR BASEBALL ITSELF, AND THE 1959 PENNANT WAS THE HIGH POINT FOR OUR TEAM."

—BILLY PIERCE, FORMER CHICAGO WHITE SOX PITCHER

FROM LEFT: WHITE SOX OUTFIELDER TED KLUSZEWSKI PHOTOS BY CHARLES GEKLER, CUBS' FIRST BASEMAN ERNIE BANKS PHOTOS BY JOE KORDICK AND SOX PITCHER BILLY PIERCE PHOTOS BY JOE KORDICK.

THE FIFTIES

SWEEPING CHANGES.
THE CHICAGO CARDINALS RUN
THROUGH A DUMMY SCRIMMAGE
AT COMISKEY PARK IN NOVEM-
BER 1950 AS PAT HARDER (42)
CLEARS THE WAY FOR CHARLIE
TRIPPI. THE CARDINALS HAD
ONLY ONE WINNING SEASON
DURING THE 1950S. AT THE END
OF THE 1959 SEASON, OWNER
VIOLET BIDWILL MOVED THE
TEAM TO ST. LOUIS.

No laughing matter.
The great thoroughbred Nashua arrives at the LaSalle Street Station in August 1955. Nashua, winner of the Preakness and Belmont Stakes, beat Kentucky Derby winner Swaps in a nationally televised match race at Washington Park. Eddie Arcaro rode Nashua to victory that day by 6 1/2 lengths, partly because Swaps was suffering from a sore foot. (Photo by Ralph Walters.) Left: Fay Blessing, chosen the Sweetest Cowgirl at the International Championship Rodeo, is lassoed by admirers at the International Amphitheatre on October 16, 1951. (Photo by Bob Kotalik.)

LEAGUE LEADERS.
SATCHEL PAIGE WARMS UP BEFORE THE EAST-WEST NEGRO AMERICAN LEAGUE ALL-STAR GAME AT COMISKEY PARK ON JULY 31, 1955. PAIGE—WHO WAS ALREADY DESCRIBED AS "AGELESS"—PITCHED THREE HITLESS INNINGS AS HIS WEST TEAM DEFEATED THE EAST 2-0. HE WAS THE FIRST NEGRO LEAGUE STAR TO BE ELECTED TO BASEBALL'S HALL OF FAME. (PHOTO BY MEL LARSON.) TOP RIGHT: JACKIE ROBINSON SIGNS A BASEBALL AS DODGERS TEAMMATE DON NEWCOMBE AND STUDENTS LOOK ON AT MOSELEY SCHOOL, 2348 SOUTH MICHIGAN AVENUE. (PHOTO BY BILL PAUER.) RIGHT: ROBINSON SIGNS AUTOGRAPHS IN THE CHRIST CONGREGATIONAL CHURCH IN OAK PARK ON JANUARY 23, 1955. (PHOTO BY LARRY NOCERINO.)

BOXING NIGHTS.
SUGAR RAY ROBINSON KNOCKS OUT CARL "BOBO" OLSON AT CHICAGO STADIUM ON DECEMBER 9, 1955, TO REGAIN THE WORLD MIDDLEWEIGHT CHAMPIONSHIP FOR THE SECOND TIME. (PHOTO BY RALPH FROST.) TOP LEFT: SUGAR RAY'S WIFE, EDNA MAY, AND HIS SISTER, EVELYN, CHEER ROBINSON DURING THE BOUT AGAINST OLSON. LEFT: CHIEF ANDY FRAIN USHER JOE "40,000" MURPHY POSES WITH A FIGHT FAN AT THE CHICAGO STADIUM IN 1957.

SUGAR'S SWEET SORROW.
VICKI LAMOTTA CRADLES HER HUSBAND, BOXER JAKE LAMOTTA, AFTER HE WAS KNOCKED OUT BY SUGAR
RAY ROBINSON. LAMOTTA LOST THE WORLD MIDDLEWEIGHT TITLE IN THE CHICAGO STADIUM FIGHT
ON FEBRUARY 14, 1951. (PHOTO BY BOB KOTALIK.) RIGHT: CARMEN BASILIO LOOKS TIRED DURING A
WORKOUT AT THE BISMARCK HOTEL ON MARCH 21, 1958. FOUR DAYS LATER, BASILIO LOST THE WORLD
MIDDLEWEIGHT TITLE TO ROBINSON, WHO BECAME THE FIRST BOXER IN HISTORY TO WIN A CHAMPIONSHIP
FIVE TIMES. (PHOTO BY CHARLES GECKLER.)

FOR THE LOVE OF IVY. PHOTOS BY JOHN ARABINKO.

CHUCK CONNORS SHOWS HIS BASKETBALL REACH AT FIRST BASE ON JULY 6, 1951. CONNORS, WHO PLAYED FOR THE BOSTON CELTICS, JOINED THE CUBS IN 1951 FOR 66 GAMES. HE WENT ON TO STAR AS LUCAS MCCAIN IN "THE RIFLEMAN" TV SERIES AND APPEAR IN MORE THAN 80 MOVIES. LEFT: AFTER THE CUBS LOST 15-8 AGAINST THE MILWAUKEE BRAVES, ROBERT BEMONT AND RONALD BRATKO HANG WID MATTHEWS IN EFFIGY AT ABERDEEN STREET AND GRAND AVENUE ON MAY 31, 1956. THE 1950S WERE THE CUBS' WORST DECADE, AND MATTHEWS—DIRECTOR OF PLAYER PERSONNEL—TOOK MUCH OF THE BLAME.

TROUBLED WATERS.

BUCK WEAVER (RIGHT), ONE OF THE BLACK SOX EIGHT, IS FETED BY FRIENDS IN 1954. UNTIL HIS DEATH 10 YEARS LATER, WEAVER MAINTAINED THAT HE NEVER ACCEPTED A BRIBE TO THROW THE 1919 WORLD SERIES. LEFT: "JUNGLE" JIM RIVERA TAKES A LIE-DETECTOR TEST ON OCTOBER 2, 1952, CLEARING HIM OF RAPE CHARGES. JOINING THE SOX OUTFIELDER WERE JOHN E. REID (LEFT), WHO CONDUCTED THE TEST, AND RIVERA'S ATTORNEY, ROBERT E. ROMANO. RIVERA WAS ACCUSED OF RAPING A 22-YEAR-OLD WOMAN. HE SAID THE SEX WAS CONSENSUAL. AFTER THE LIE TEST, HE WAS CLEARED BY A GRAND JURY BUT GIVEN "INDEFINITE PROBATION" BY BASEBALL COMMISSIONER FORD FRICK, WHO SAID, "WE WANT TO KEEP A CLOSE EYE ON HIM THE REST OF HIS BASEBALL CAREER." (PHOTO BY RALPH WALTERS.)

KINGS OF THE RING.
GORGEOUS GEORGE IS NOT SO GORGEOUS AS HE LEAVES THE RING AFTER A REFEREE STOPPED HIS
WRESTLING MATCH AGAINST CHAMP LOU THESZ AT WRIGLEY FIELD ON JULY 27, 1950. (PHOTO BY
JOHN PAGORIA.) RIGHT: CHICAGO'S MAX MAREK, WHO BEAT JOE LOUIS IN THE FINALS OF THE 1933
NATIONAL A.A.U. LIGHT-HEAVYWEIGHT BOXING TOURNAMENT, RETURNED TO THE RING AS A WRES-
TLER IN THE 1950S.

MODERN WOMEN.
FLORENCE NELSON ACCEPTS THE WINNER'S FLAG FROM PETE PASSENTINO AFTER NELSON WON THE WOMEN'S STOCK CAR RACE AT THE SANTA FE SPEEDWAY IN WILLOW SPRINGS IN 1956. (PHOTO BY RALPH ARVIDSON.) TOP: MARY LOU PALERMO, OF THE CHICAGO WESTERNERS, RELAXES DURING A BREAK FROM THE ROLLER DERBY AT THE COLISEUM IN 1954. (PHOTO BY RALPH ARVIDSON.) LEFT: SYLVIA WENE HAS TO REACH TO THE TOP OF THE SHELF TO GET A BOWLING BALL IN 1957. TWO YEARS LATER AT THE COLISEUM, SHE BOWLED THE FIRST SANCTIONED PERFECT GAME IN WOMEN'S MATCH PLAY. (PHOTO BY JOE KORDICK.)

ALL DOWNHILL FROM HERE.
JOAN PORTER, OF CHICAGO, TRIES OUT THE WILMOT SKI SLOPE IN WISCONSIN ON JANUARY 30, 1955. OWN-
ERS OF THE SKI HILL BEGAN MAKING ARTIFICIAL SNOW IN THE EARLY 1950S, CREATING A FULL-TIME WINTER
SKI OPERATION THAT ATTRACTED CHICAGOANS TO THE SPORT. (PHOTO BY HOWARD LYON.) LEFT: A SPRINGER
SPANIEL NAMED SUSIE WAITS FOR HER MASTER AT A GUN CLUB NEAR SUBURBAN VOLO ON OCTOBER 20, 1954.
(PHOTO BY BILL STURM.)

'WHEN LAD NEEDS FRIEND.' PHOTO BY RALPH WALTERS, NOVEMBER 28, 1957
PAT STANTON, 9, SWEEPS TO THE LEFT AT PAUL REVERE PARK, 2501 WEST IRVING PARK ROAD, DUR-
ING A MIGHTY MITES FOOTBALL GAME. THE PARK HOSTED 30 TEAMS AT A THANKSGIVING FOOTBALL
FEST. THE PHOTOGRAPHER WROTE, "IMPOSSIBLE TO GET KIDS' NAMES; GOT SCOLDED FOR GETTING
HIS, AND WASTING THEIR TIME."

A COACHABLE MOMENT. PHOTO BY BOB KOTALIK, NOVEMBER 29, 1952
AUSTIN HIGH SCHOOL RUNNING BACK ABE WOODSON IS CONSOLED BY HIS COACH, BILL HEILAND,
AS HIS TEAM LOST TO MOUNT CARMEL IN THE PREP BOWL AT SOLDIER FIELD. MOUNT CARMEL WON
AN UNPRECEDENTED THIRD STRAIGHT CITY CHAMPIONSHIP. WOODSON, ONE OF THE CITY'S FIRST AF-
RICAN AMERICAN FOOTBALL STARS, WENT ON TO BECOME AN NFL PRO BOWL DEFENSIVE BACK.

FUTURE MONSTER. PHOTO BY GENE PESEK, NOVEMBER 29, 1959
DICK BUTKUS, KNOWN AS RICH BUTKUS AT THE TIME, JOINS HIS MOTHER, EMMA; FATHER, JOHN, AND
CHICAGO VOCATIONAL HIGH SCHOOL COACH BERNIE O'BRIEN AT THE BUTKUS HOME AT 10324 SOUTH
LOWE. THE "EARTHSHAKING FULLBACK," WHO ALSO PLAYED DEFENSE, WAS NAMED SUN-TIMES PLAYER
OF THE YEAR AS A JUNIOR. HE MADE 70 PERCENT OF THE TEAM'S TACKLES.

WILDCAT WHOOPEE. PHOTO BY BILL STURM, NOVEMBER 1, 1958
NORTHWESTERN UNIVERSITY FOOTBALL COACH ARA PARSEGHIAN LEADS THE CHEERS AS THE WILD-
CATS BEAT UNDEFEATED OHIO STATE 21-0 AT EVANSTON'S DYCHE STADIUM BEFORE A HOMECOMING
CROWD OF MORE THAN 51,000 FANS. THE TEAM HAD NOT BEATEN OHIO STATE SINCE 1948.

READY FOR THE BIG SHOW.
COACH-OWNER GEORGE HALAS LOADS HIS BEARS ONTO A BUS FOR SUMMER PRACTICE AT RENSSELAER, INDIANA, IN 1955. THE BEARS WON EIGHT GAMES AND LOST FOUR THAT YEAR, THE SAME RECORD THEY HAD IN 1954. (PHOTO BY BILL STURM.) RIGHT: AN AERIAL VIEW OF WRIGLEY FIELD SHORTLY AFTER THE BEARS BEAT THE RAMS 31-10 ON OCTOBER 19, 1958. (PHOTO BY BOB KOTALIK.)

PICTURE THIS. JULY 31, 1958

ON PICTURE DAY, ALL OF THE RUNNING HOLES ARE HUGE, ALL OF THE PASSES ARE PERFECT, AND ALL OF THE CUTS ARE GRACEFUL. ABOVE: JIM GLOVER (FROM LEFT), MERRILL DOUGLAS AND TED KARRAS BUST OPEN A LONG GAIN. TOP RIGHT: QUARTERBACKS GEORGE BLANDA (FROM LEFT), ED BROWN AND ZEKE BRATKOWSKI SHOW THEIR FORM. RIGHT: HALFBACK WILLIE GALIMORE HIGH STEPS. GALIMORE DIED IN A CAR CRASH ALONG WITH OFFENSIVE END JOHN FARRINGTON AS THEY DROVE TO PRACTICE IN 1964.

THE SOFT SHOE. PHOTO BY MERRILL PALMER, AUGUST 9, 1955
JOCKEY WILLIE SHOEMAKER TENDS TO SWAPS AT WASHINGTON PARK IN PREPARATION FOR HIS MATCH RACE AGAINST NASHUA. "SWAPS IS THE BEST I EVER RODE," HE SAID AT THE TIME. A WEEK LATER, SWAPS TOOK THE AMERICAN DERBY AT WASHINGTON PARK BEFORE HIS MATCH-RACE LOSS TO NASHUA.

A PICTURE OF CONFIDENCE. PHOTO BY MICKEY RITO, SEPTEMBER 10, 1956
JACK NICKLAUS, 17, COMPETES IN THE 56TH NATIONAL AMATEUR GOLF TOURNAMENT AT THE KNOLLWOOD
CLUB IN SUBURBAN LAKE FOREST. NICKLAUS WON THE FIRST TWO ROUNDS OF MATCH PLAY BEFORE BOW-
ING OUT. HE WENT ON TO WIN TWO U.S. AMATEUR CHAMPIONSHIPS BEFORE HIS PROFESSIONAL CAREER.

IN COMMANDO. PHOTO BY BOB KOTALIK.
MARSHALL'S GEORGE WILSON LED THE COMMANDOS TO THE STATE BASKETBALL CHAMPIONSHIP IN 1958 AND 1960. THE ALL-BLACK TEAM WAS THE FIRST CHICAGO PUBLIC LEAGUE SCHOOL TO WIN THE STATE TITLE. WILSON WENT ON TO PLAY COLLEGE AND PROFESSIONAL BASKETBALL, AND WIN A GOLD MEDAL ON THE 1964 UNITED STATES OLYMPIC BASKETBALL TEAM.

SHOULD HE SIGN IT? PHOTO BY BILL KNEFEL, MARCH 27, 1959
RAY MEYER SHOWS HIS NEW DEPAUL CONTRACT TO HIS WIFE, MARGE, AND CHILDREN. THEY ARE (FROM LEFT): JOEY, 9; PATRICIA, 13; MARY ANN, 11; BARBARA, 16; RAY, 15, AND ROBERT, 6. RAY MEYER COACHED AT DEPAUL UNIVERSITY FOR 42 YEARS, COMPILING THE SIXTH-BEST RECORD IN NCAA HISTORY. IN 1959, MEYER CONSIDERED SWITCHING TO THE UNIVERSITY OF WISCONSIN. JOEY, HIS SON AND LONGTIME ASSISTANT, TOOK OVER THE TEAM AFTER RAY RETIRED IN 1984, AND COACHED DEPAUL FOR 13 SEASONS.

THE ROAD TO THE GAMES.

THE 1959 UNITED STATES PAN AMERICAN BASKETBALL TEAM WORKS OUT AS THE GAMES COME TO CHICAGO. THEY ARE (FROM LEFT) BOB BOOZER, JERRY WEST, TRAINER AL SAWDY, OSCAR ROBERTSON, GARY THOMPSON AND GEORGE BONSALLE. THEY WON ALL SIX GAMES. TOP: THE BATTERY-POWERED FRIENDSHIP TORCH OF THE PAN AMERICAN GAMES IS CARRIED NORTH TOWARD CHICAGO BY BOY SCOUTS ALONG ROUTE 66. (PHOTO BY EDWARD DELUGA.) RIGHT: JESSE OWENS TRIES OUT THE SOLDIER FIELD TRACK BEFORE THE GAMES BEGAN. (PHOTO BY EDWARD DELUGA.)

THE GAMES IN CHICAGO. CLOCKWISE FROM TOP LEFT: OPENING CEREMONY AT PORTAGE PARK ON AUGUST 31, 1959. (PHOTO BY DAVE MANN.) RIDERS TAKE PART IN THE MODERN PENTATHLON. (PHOTO BY BOB KOTALIK.) BICYCLISTS PEDDLE NEAR LAKE SHORE DRIVE AND FOSTER AVENUE. (PHOTO BY BILL STURM.) UNITED STATES' RUNNERS ALFRED CONFALONE (LEFT) AND JAMES GREEN MAKE THE BIG TURN ON THE LAKE SHORE DRIVE S-CURVE DURING THE MARATHON. (PHOTO BY BOB KOTALIK.) LEFT: CASSIUS CLAY PRACTICES HIS PUNCHES. CLAY'S STREAK OF 36 CONSECUTIVE AMATEUR VICTORIES WAS BROKEN WHEN HE LOST IN THE FINALS OF THE PAN AMERICAN GAMES TRIALS. HE NEVER LOST AN AMATEUR FIGHT AGAIN.

LADIES . . . PHOTOS BY BOB KOTALIK, AUGUST 20, 1959
WOMEN ROOT ON THEIR FAVORITE TEAM ON LADIES DAY AT COMISKEY PARK.

. . . **AND THEIR MEN.** CLOCKWISE FROM TOP LEFT: WHITE SOX NELLIE FOX, MAN-
AGER AL LOPEZ, BILLY PIERCE, LUIS APARICIO, EARLY WYNN AND JIM LANDIS.

LET'S GO-GO WHITE SOX.
AL SMITH DOUBLES OFF THE LEFT-FIELD WALL, SCORING EARL TORGESON AND ADVANCING SHERM LOLLAR IN
THE EIGHTH INNING OF GAME 2 OF THE WORLD SERIES ON OCTOBER 3, 1959. DESPITE HIS GOOD LEAD OFF
FIRST BASE, LOLLAR WAS THROWN OUT AT THE PLATE. THE RUN WOULD HAVE TIED THE SCORE. INSTEAD, THE SOX
LOST 4-3 AS THE DODGERS TIED THE SERIES. LEFT PHOTOS: SOX FANS WHOOP IT UP AS THE TEAM CLINCHES THE
PENNANT ON SEPTEMBER 22, 1959. TOP: IN A TAVERN AT 3423 SOUTH RACINE AVENUE. BOTTOM: IN FRONT OF
COMISKEY PARK. (PHOTOS BY MERRILL PALMER.)

BEER AND CHEERS.
THE DODGERS CELEBRATE THEIR 4 GAMES TO 2 WORLD SERIES VICTORY AFTER BEATING THE SOX AT COMISKEY PARK ON OCTOBER 8, 1959. COACH JOE BECKER (33) GETS A BEER BATH FROM WALLY MOON (FROM LEFT), PEE WEE REESE AND DON DRYSDALE. (PHOTO BY BOB KOTALIK.) LEFT PHOTO: SOX SLUGGER TED KLUSZEWSKI CROSSES HOME AFTER HIS SECOND HOME RUN IN GAME 1. "THAT WASN'T TOO BAD FOR A START, BUT WHAT DO I DO FOR AN ENCORE?" HE ASKED FANS AFTER THE GAME. (PHOTO BY DAVE MANN.)

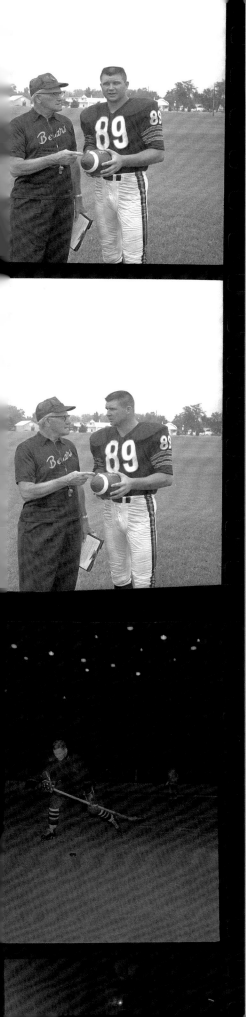

"YOU KNOW, WHEN YOU GROW UP ON THE PRAIRIES OF SASKATCHEWAN, CANADA, THERE AREN'T THAT MANY PEOPLE.

"WHEN I WAS YOUNG, WE DIDN'T TRAVEL MUCH. I DIDN'T TRAVEL HARDLY AT ALL UNTIL I WENT TO COLLEGE IN COLORADO. THEN I CAME TO CHICAGO.

"CHICAGO WAS A BIG CITY FOR ME. I HAD TWO YOUNG CHILDREN AT THE TIME, AND I HAD A WIFE FROM THE PRAIRIES. NATURALLY, CHICAGO'S SIZE AND ITS PACE FRIGHTENED US A LITTLE BIT.

"WE DIDN'T KNOW ANY PEOPLE IN THE CITY, SO WE BECAME VERY CLOSE WITH TEAMMATES AND THEIR FAMILIES. MOST OF THE HAWKS AND THEIR FAMILIES LIVED IN THE WESTERN SUBURBS, IN AREAS LIKE BELLWOOD WHERE WE WOULD RENT HOMES. THEY WERE MOSTLY OLD BUNGALOWS AND APARTMENTS, AND WE LIVED CLOSE TO EACH OTHER.

"WE DIDN'T LIVE IN THE LOOP BECAUSE MOST OF US WERE MARRIED WITH YOUNG, GROWING FAMILIES, AND WE SELDOM EVEN WENT DOWNTOWN. MONDAY NIGHT WAS THE ONLY TIME WE HAD OFF, AND THAT WAS A FAMILY NIGHT. WHEN THE SEASON ENDED, WE ALL WENT BACK TO OUR HOMES IN CANADA. I HAD A JOB IN THE OIL INDUSTRY. I GOT THERE THE DAY AFTER THE SEASON ENDED, AND I WAS ANXIOUS TO GET TO WORK. MOST OF THE PLAYERS HAD TO WORK DURING THE SUMMER, AND I'M GLAD I DID. IT REALLY GROOMED ME FOR MY CAREER AFTER RETIREMENT FROM HOCKEY.

"AS FOR MY FIRST IMPRESSIONS OF THE CHICAGO STADIUM AND THE CITY AFTER I GOT HERE, IT WAS REALLY QUITE EXCITING. WE WOULD TRAIN IN ST. CATHERINE'S, ONTARIO, IN A LITTLE RINK WITH A CAPACITY OF AROUND 2,500 PEOPLE. THEN WE MOVED INTO THE STADIUM, WHICH WAS BIGGER THAN ANYTHING I HAD EVER SEEN IN MY LIFE. I REMEMBER WE WOULD SORT OF STARE UP AT IT WHEN IT WAS EMPTY, AND THEN, WHEN IT WAS FULL WE GOT A THRILL BECAUSE ALL OF THE FANS WERE ON OUR SIDE. WE REALLY WANTED TO PERFORM FOR THEM. THE CHICAGO STADIUM WAS AN OLD BUILDING, BUT AN EXCITING PLACE.

"CHICAGO FANS WERE SPECIAL BECAUSE THEY WEREN'T SELF-CENTERED. WE HAD A FAN CLUB, AND WE VISITED WITH THEM. WE DIDN'T WEAR HELMETS IN THOSE DAYS, AND WE DIDN'T DRIVE INTO THE BASEMENT OF THE RINK IN A DARK, TINTED BUS. WE WERE WITH THE FANS, AND THEY ENJOYED THAT.

"CHICAGO PEOPLE STILL REMEMBER THE BLACKHAWKS OF THE '60S AS I TRAVEL AROUND THE WORLD. THEY LOVED THE SIX-TEAM STRUCTURE OF HOCKEY IN THOSE DAYS AND THE 'MILLION DOLLAR LINE.' THEY LOVED OUR STARS, LIKE BOBBY HULL, STAN MIKITA AND GLENN HALL, WHO WERE JUST COMING INTO THEIR OWN. WE WERE AN EXCITING TEAM, AND THE FANS CAME ALONG WITH US."

—BILL "RED" HAY, CHICAGO BLACKHAWKS CENTER

FROM LEFT: CUBS MANAGER LEO DUROCHER PHOTOS BY BOB LANGER, GOLFER ARNOLD PALMER PHOTOS BY EDWARD DELUGA, BEARS COACH GEORGE HALAS AND TIGHT END MIKE DITKA PHOTOS BY BUD DALEY, AND BLACKHAWKS CENTER BILL HAY PHOTO BY BOB KOTALIK.

THE SIXTIES

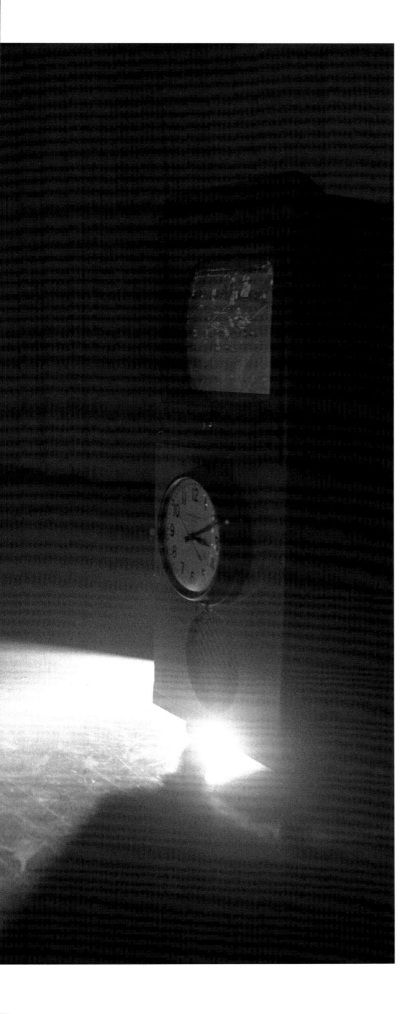

SUPER SCOUTS. PHOTO BY LOUIS GIAMPA,
NOVEMBER 6, 1960
BEARS OWNER GEORGE HALAS (SITTING) AND
ASSISTANT SID LUCKMAN WATCH THE GREEN
BAY PACKERS PLAY THE BALTIMORE COLTS ON
A SPECIAL CLOSED-CIRCUIT TELECAST PROVIDED
FOR THEM AT THE CBS STUDIOS IN CHICAGO.
THE BEARS PLAYED BOTH TEAMS LATER IN THE
SEASON—AND LOST BOTH GAMES.

NO MORE FIREWORKS. PHOTO BY BUD DALEY, APRIL 7, 1961
WHITE SOX PRESIDENT BILL VEECK, WHO GUIDED THE SOX TO THE PENNANT IN 1959, SURVEYS HIS COMISKEY
PARK TURF PRIOR TO THE PRESEASON CITY SERIES. TWO MONTHS LATER, VEECK SOLD HIS SHARE OF THE TEAM
AND RETIRED DUE TO POOR HEALTH. BUT VEECK RETURNED IN 1975 AS FULL OWNER.

THE GO-GO GUY IS GONE. PHOTO BY MERRILL PALMER, NOVEMBER 27, 1961
MINNIE MINOSO AND HIS WIFE, EDELIA, PAUSE IN THEIR SOUTH SIDE HOME AFTER MINOSO LEARNED HE WAS
TRADED TO THE ST. LOUIS CARDINALS. "HE'LL BE MISSED NOT SO MUCH BECAUSE OF HIS HITTING," WROTE
THE SUN-TIMES, "BUT BECAUSE HE SYMBOLIZED THE SPEED AND AGGRESSIVENESS THAT HAS BECOME A WHITE
SOX TRADEMARK."

PLAYING IN LEFT FIELD. JULY 22, 1964
YOUNG SOX FANS WATCH A GAME FROM THE COMISKEY PARK PICNIC AREA BENEATH THE OUTFIELD
STANDS. IT WAS A PLACE WHERE YOU COULD EAT A HOT DOG, DRINK A BEER AND MUNCH ON A CHURRO
WHILE RAZZING THE LEFT FIELDER.

SEASON OF CHANGE. PHOTO BY EDMUND JARECKI, AUGUST 4, 1964
A FIVE-GAME WINNING STREAK COMES TO AN END WHEN DETROIT TIGER DOM DEMETER SLAMS A THREE-RUN HOMER IN THE EIGHTH INNING AGAINST THE SOX AT COMISKEY. THE SOX WERE AT THEIR APOGEE THAT SEASON, POSTING A 98-64 RECORD, BUT FELL A GAME BACK TO THE YANKEES FOR THE PENNANT.

MR. ALDERMAN. PHOTO BY ELLIOTT ROBINSON, FEBRUARY 1, 1963
ERNIE BANKS CAMPAIGNS AS HE RUNS FOR EIGTHTH WARD ALDERMAN ON THE SOUTH SIDE. BANKS RAN AS AN INDEPEN-
DENT. "THE ELECTION IS FEBRUARY 26. I'M LEAVING THE NEXT DAY FOR SPRING TRAINING AS ALDERMAN," HE CHARAC-
TERISTICALLY TOLD A REPORTER. BANKS LOST TO ALDERMAN JAMES CONDON 9,296-2,028.

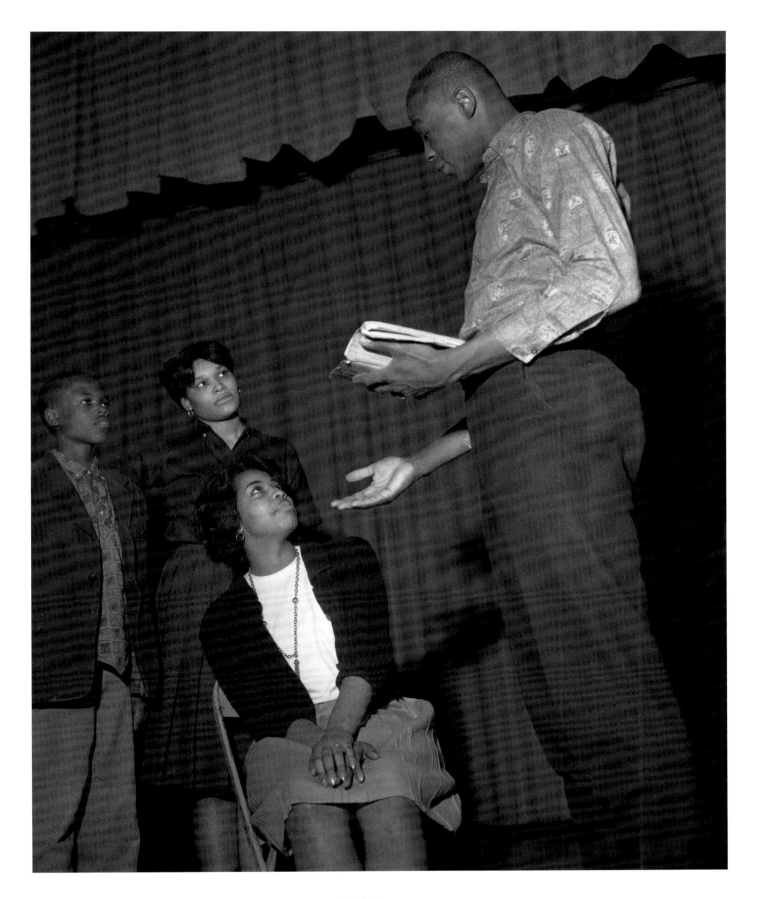

ALWAYS A ROLE PLAYER. PHOTO BY MEL LARSON, APRIL 2, 1962
BASKETBALL STAR CAZZIE RUSSELL REHEARSES THE PLAY "A RAISIN IN THE SUN" AT CARVER HIGH SCHOOL. RUSSELL WAS
DISCOVERED—AS A BASKETBALL PLAYER—WHILE IN FRESHMAN GYM CLASS BY CARVER COACH LARRY HAWKINS. RUSSELL
WENT ON TO BECOME ONE OF THE BEST HIGH SCHOOL PLAYERS IN CITY HISTORY AS WELL AS A COLLEGE AND NBA STAR.

THE NEW ORDER.
ROGER MARIS PRACTICES UNDER THE COMISKEY PARK LIGHTS ON SEPTEMBER 15, 1961. MARIS CAME TO CHICAGO WITH 56 HOMERS AND LEFT WITH ONLY SINGLES IN THREE GAMES. HE WOULD END THE SEASON WITH 61 HOMERS AND AN ASTERISK. LEFT: CASSIUS CLAY TAKES ONE ON THE CHIN ON JULY 16, 1963, AT A RESTAURANT NEAR O'HARE AIRPORT. HE WOULD WIN THE WORLD CHAMPIONSHIP AND CHANGE HIS NAME THE FOLLOWING YEAR. (PHOTO BY RALPH WALTERS.)

TEED OFF. PHOTOS BY BUD DALEY.
GOLFER SAM SNEAD TAKES AIM IN WRIGLEY FIELD WITH THE HELP OF CUBS PITCHER DON CARDWELL ON JULY 6, 1961. TEN YEARS EARLIER, SNEAD STRUCK THE CUBS SCOREBOARD WITH A LAZY 4-IRON FROM HOME PLATE AND THEN CLEARED THE SCOREBOARD WITH A 2-IRON. (PHOTO BY BUD DALEY.) LEFT: GARY PLAYER (LEFT) AND ARNOLD PALMER PEEK OUT OF THE CLUBHOUSE TO CHECK ON THE RAIN AT THE PGA CHAMPIONSHIP AT OLYMPIA FIELDS COUNTRY CLUB ON JULY 18, 1961. THE TOURNAMENT WAS WON BY JERRY BARBER.

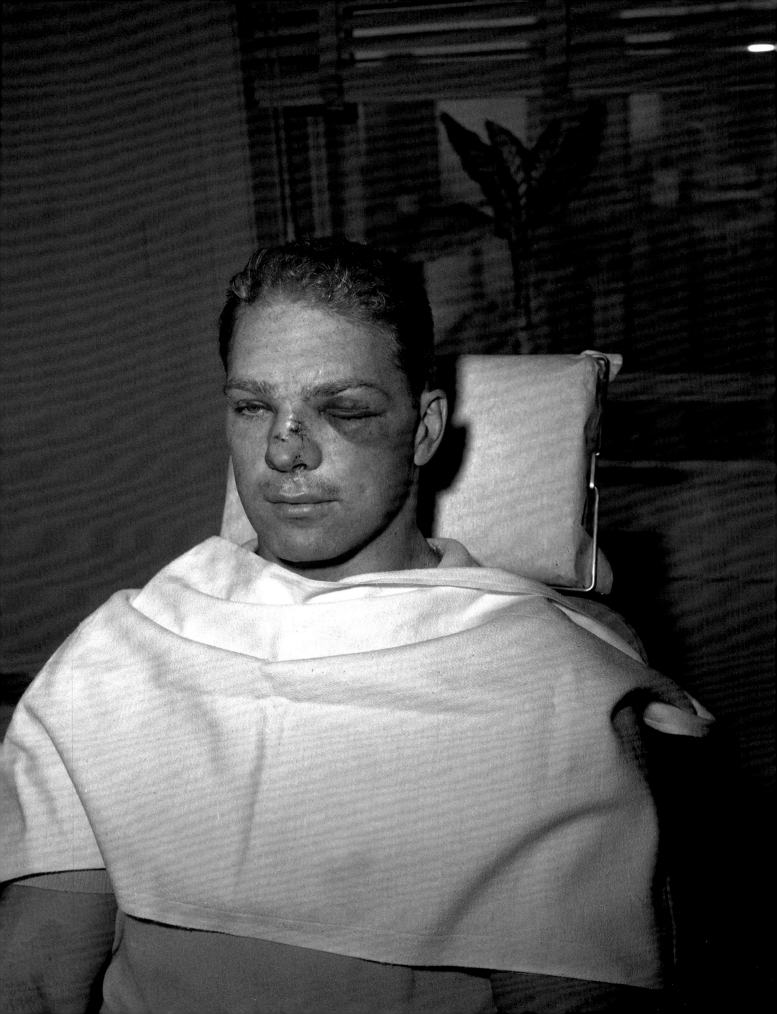

SPIRIT OF THE BLACKHAWKS. PHOTOS BY JOE KORDICK.
STAN MIKITA SHARPENS HIS SKATES ON FEBRUARY 14, 1963. HE SERVED AS A MAINSTAY OF THE HAWKS FROM 1958 TO 1980. LEFT: BOBBY HULL WAITS IN THE EXAMINING ROOM OF HIS DOCTOR ON MARCH 23, 1963. BESIDES THE FACIAL INJURY, HULL SAID HE COULD NOT RAISE HIS ARM WITHOUT PAIN. HE SAID HE WOULD MISS THE FIRST GAME OR TWO OF THE STANLEY CUP SERIES, BUT HE PLAYED IN THE OPENER THREE DAYS LATER AND SCORED TWO GOALS.

STANLEY CUP CHAMPS.

A FIGHT BREAKS OUT BETWEEN THE BLACKHAWKS AND MONTREAL CANADIENS DURING THE STANLEY CUP PLAYOFFS AT THE CHICAGO STADIUM ON MARCH 28, 1961. THE HAWKS LOST THE GAME, BUT WON THE PLAYOFF SERIES 4 GAMES TO 2. (PHOTO BY MICKEY RITO.) TOP RIGHT: WITH VICTORY LESS THAN A MINUTE AWAY, HAWKS' COACH RUDY PILOUS BARKS OUT DIRECTIONS ON APRIL 4, 1961. THE HAWKS ENDED A LOSING STREAK OF FIVE SEASON-ENDING PLAYOFF SERIES AGAINST THE CANADIENS DATING BACK TO 1944. IN THE BACKGROUND ARE ERIC NESTERENKO (15) AND ED LITZENBERGER. (PHOTO BY LUTHER JOSEPH.) RIGHT: AFTER BEATING THE DETROIT RED WINGS FOR THE STANLEY CUP, HAWKS PLAYERS VIEW THEIR PRIZE ON APRIL 17, 1961, AT THE BISMARCK HOTEL. THEY ARE (FROM LEFT) BOBBY HULL, REG FLEMING AND PIERRE PILOTE. (PHOTO BY MEL LARSON.)

Brrrr down, Chicago Bears. December 29, 1963
Some 45,801 football fans bundle up in 8-degree weather to watch the Bears take on the New York Giants for the NFL Championship at Wrigley Field.

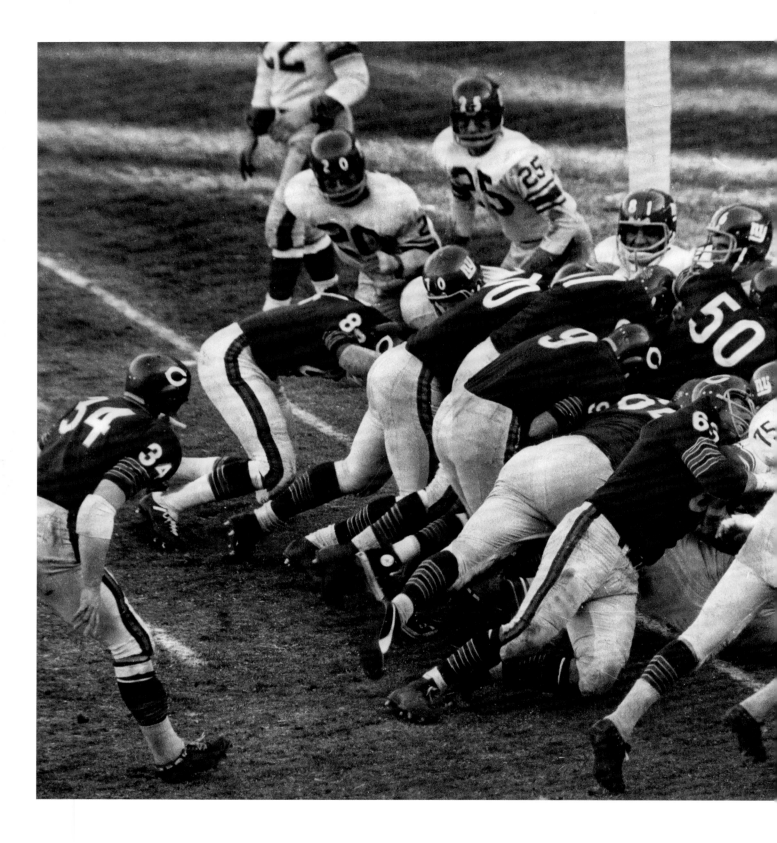

BACK ON TOP. DECEMBER 29, 1963

BEARS QUARTERBACK BILL WADE, BEHIND A BATTERING RAM OF TEAMMATES, MAKES IT ACROSS THE GOAL LINE
FOR THE BEARS' SECOND TOUCHDOWN. TOP RIGHT: INJURED GIANTS QUARTERBACK Y.A. TITTLE IS HELPED
OFF THE FIELD IN THE SECOND QUARTER. TITTLE CAME BACK TO TRY AGAIN—BUT HE TOSSED A TOTAL OF FIVE
INTERCEPTIONS. RIGHT: GEORGE HALAS EMBRACES WADE AFTER THE GAME. IT WAS HALAS' SIXTH AND LAST
CHAMPIONSHIP. (PHOTO BY RALPH ARVIDSON.)

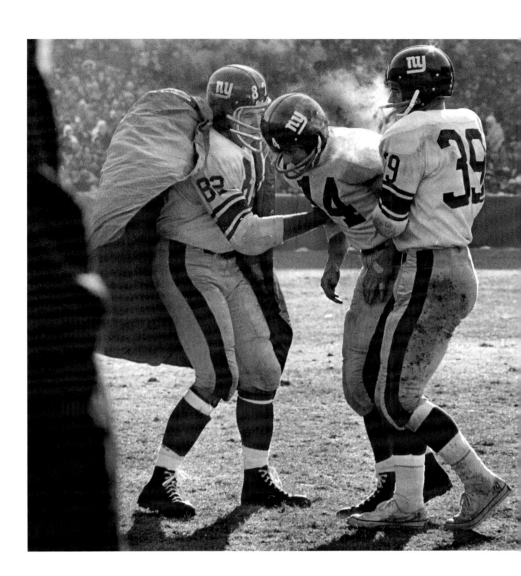

CHICAGO PRIDE.

THE LOYOLA RAMBLERS POSE IN ALUMNI GYM AFTER RETURNING TO CHICAGO WITH THE NCAA CHAMPIONSHIP IN 1963. IN THE FRONT ROW ARE HEAD COACH GEORGE IRELAND (LEFT) AND ASSISTANT COACH JERRY LYNE. IN THE BACK ROW ARE (FROM LEFT) JERRY HARKNESS, JOHN EGAN, CHUCK WOOD, VIC ROUSE, LES HUNTER, RICH ROCHELLE, JIM REARDON, DAN CONNAUGHTON, RON MILLER, MANAGER JOHN GABCIK, MANAGER FRED KUEHL AND TRAINER DENNIS MCKENNA. RIGHT: HARLEM GLOBETROTTERS OWNER-COACH ABE SAPERSTEIN POSES WITH BILL GARNER (LEFT) AND CONNIE HAWKINS AT A NORTH SIDE GYM ON OCTOBER 21, 1963. HAWKINS WENT ON TO STAR IN THE ORIGINAL AMERICAN BASKETBALL ASSOCIATION AND NATIONAL BASKETBALL ASSOCIATION. THE GLOBETROTTERS—DESPITE ITS NAME—STARTED IN CHICAGO. (PHOTO BY MEL LARSON.)

RUNNING OF THE SMELT. PHOTO BY JACK LENAHAN, APRIL 15, 1964
IRVING KLAGES AND WILLIAM PAFF SET UP THEIR GILL NET TO START THE SMELT FISHING SEASON AT 30TH STREET AND LAKE MICHIGAN. SILVERY RAINBOW SMELT WERE FIRST REPORTED IN THE LAKE IN 1923, AND THEY STARTED TO REACH HIGH LEVELS IN THE 1940S. THE BEST SMELT FISHING USUALLY LASTS ABOUT A WEEK IN MID-APRIL, AS THE TINY FISH HEAD TO THE LAKESHORE TO SPAWN—AND BECOME DINNER FOOD.

DISTANT COMPETITOR. JULY 21, 1967
A VIEW FROM THE YACHT RUBAIYAT AS IT HEADS NORTH IN LAKE MICHIGAN FROM CHICAGO TO MACKINAC
ISLAND, MICHIGAN. THE 1967 MAC RACE WAS THE LARGEST AND ONE OF THE FASTEST TO DATE. SOME
163 BOATS EMBARKED ON THE 333-MILE JOURNEY, AND ALL BUT TWO FINISHED.

FULL HOUSES AT WRIGLEY. PHOTO BY BOB LANGER.
AFTER YEARS OF LOSING TEAMS AND LOW ATTENDANCE, THE CUBS PLAY TO CAPACITY CROWDS IN
AUGUST 1967. IT WAS THE TEAM'S FIRST TIME IN THE FIRST DIVISION SINCE 1946.

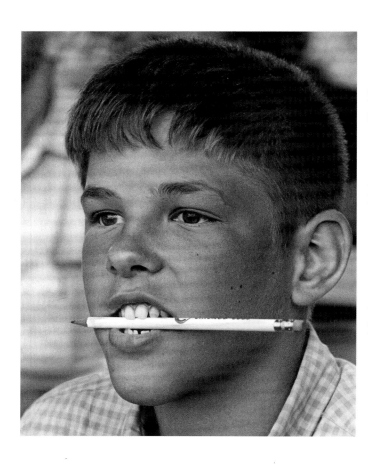

A YOUNG MAN'S GAME.
A FAN HANGS ON TO A WRIGLEY FIELD RAILING FOR A BETTER VIEW OF FERGUSON JENKINS IN 1967.
LEFT: PHOTOGRAPHER BOB KOTALIK TURNED HIS CAMERA ON THE CUBS' YOUNGEST ROOTERS IN 1966.

BREAKAWAY BEAR.
GALE SAYERS, THE MOST GRACEFUL RUNNER TO PUT ON A BEARS UNIFORM, USES BLOCKS FROM DICK GORDON (45) AND JOHNNY MORRIS (47) AS HE SET OFF ON A 70-YARD RUN AGAINST THE DETROIT LIONS ON OCTOBER 16, 1967. (PHOTO BY DON BIERMAN.) RIGHT: SAYERS IS GREETED BY FANS NEAR THE WRIGLEY FIELD IVY AFTER A 43-YARD TOUCHDOWN RUN ON NOVEMBER 27, 1967. INJURIES CUT SAYERS' CAREER SHORT. (PHOTO BY GARY SETTLE.)

BABY BULLS. PHOTO BY HOWARD LYON, AUGUST 12, 1966
FIRST CHICAGO BULLS COACH JOHNNY "RED" KERR WATCHES HIS ROOKIES SCRIMMAGE AT DEPAUL'S ALUMNI
HALL. THE BULLS' OPENING NIGHT LINEUP INCLUDED BOB BOOZER, JERRY SLOAN, GUY RODGERS, DON KOJIS
AND LEN CHAPPELL. CHICAGO'S NEWEST MAJOR SPORTS FRANCHISE BECAME THE FIRST EXPANSION TEAM IN
HISTORY TO MAKE THE PLAYOFFS. KERR WAS NAMED NBA COACH OF THE YEAR.

RIGHT: FIRST SEASON CHAMPIONSHIP. PHOTO BY DAVE FORNELL, MARCH 12, 1967
BLACKHAWKS COACH BILLY REAY IS HOISTED ON THE SHOULDERS OF STAN MIKITA AND OTHER PLAYERS AFTER
THE TEAM WON ITS FIRST REGULAR SEASON CHAMPIONSHIP. BUT THE HAWKS LOST TO THE TORONTO MAPLE
LEAFS IN THE FIRST ROUND OF THE STANLEY CUP PLAYOFFS.

THE TIMES WERE A CHANGIN'.
CUBS SHORTSTOP DON KESSINGER REPORTS FOR ACTIVE DUTY IN THE U.S. ARMY RESERVES AT FORT SHERIDAN ON MARCH 4, 1968. "I DIDN'T GIVE IT MUCH THOUGHT, IT WAS JUST MY OBLIGATION," SAID KESSINGER OF HIS TERM OF SERVICE. THE VIETNAM WAR AND CONCERNS OF THE '60S SELDOM OVERLAPPED BASEBALL. "FOR A LOT OF PEOPLE, WRIGLEY FIELD WAS A RELIEF," HE SAID. (PHOTO BY ED DELUGA.) RIGHT: FAR AWAY FROM WRIGLEY FIELD, BASEBALLS WERE USED AS WEAPONS. HERE, CHICAGO POLICE SHOW A SPIKED BALL THAT WAS SUPPOSEDLY USED BY DEMONSTRATORS AT THE 1968 DEMOCRATIC NATIONAL CONVENTION.

ARLINGTON AT NIGHT. PHOTOS BY HOWARD SIMMONS, AUGUST 29, 1969
RACE FANS GATHER TO WATCH—AND WAGER ON—NIGHT RACING AT ARLINGTON PARK. IT MARKED A NEW ERA IN
THOROUGHBRED RACING AS ARLINGTON BECAME THE FIRST MAJOR TRACK IN THE NATION TO RUN AT NIGHT. SAID
JOCKEY WILLIE SHOEMAKER, WHO RODE TWO WINNERS UNDER THE LIGHTS, "THIS IS THE COMING THING."

A CHICAGO ORIGINAL. PHOTOS BY DON BIERMAN, AUGUST 5, 1969
TEAMS SQUARE OFF IN KELLY PARK, 4100 SOUTH CALIFORNIA AVENUE FOR A NIGHT OF SOFTBALL—OF THE 16-INCH
VARIETY. REPORTER BOB BILLINGS OBSERVED THAT THE CHICAGO SPORT IS UNIQUE IN THAT IT FAVORS AGE OVER
YOUTH. "SOFTBALL IS AN OLD MAN'S GAME," HE WROTE, "BECAUSE A PLAYER HAS TO MAKE ABOUT 50,000 OUTS BE-
FORE HE GETS SMART ENOUGH TO STOP TRYING TO HIT THE BIG, FAT, SLOW-PITCHED CUSHION OUT OF SIGHT."

THE FEEL OF THE GAME.
RUTH SHUMAN, A BLIND WOMAN WHO WAS A CUBS FAN SINCE 1957, MEETS CUBS CATCHER RANDY HUND-
LEY BEFORE A GAME ON JULY 26, 1969. (PHOTO BY JOE KORDICK.) LEFT: ERNIE BANKS SIGNS AUTOGRAPHS
ON OPENING DAY, APRIL 8, 1969. BANKS HIT TWO HOMERS IN ONE OF THE MOST EXCITING OPENERS IN CUBS
HISTORY, AS THE TEAM BEAT THE PHILADELPHIA PHILLIES ON A PINCH-HIT HOME RUN BY WILLIE SMITH IN
THE ELEVENTH INNING. (PHOTO BY BOB LANGER.)

WHAT A SEASON!
THE 1969 CUBS SEASON WILL BE REMEMBERED BY MANY CUBS FANS AS BOTH THE ALL-TIME BEST AND ALL-TIME WORST. FAR OUT IN FIRST PLACE IN AUGUST, THE TEAM SPIRALED TO A DISHEARTENING SECOND-PLACE FINISH, BUT LEFT MANY MEMORIES. ABOVE: BILLY WILLIAMS IS GIVEN A CHRYSLER IMPERIAL—AS WELL AS A WASHER AND DRYER—ON JUNE 29, THE DAY HE BROKE THE NATIONAL LEAGUE RECORD FOR CONSECUTIVE GAMES PLAYED. (PHOTO BY BOB LANGER.) TOP LEFT: RON SANTO CLICKS HIS HEELS—A VICTORY DANCE—ON AUGUST 1. (PHOTO BY PERRY C. RIDDLE.) BOTTOM LEFT: KEN HOLTZMAN GREETS WELL-WISHERS AFTER PITCHING A NO-HITTER ON AUGUST 19, 1969. (PHOTO BY BOB LANGER.)

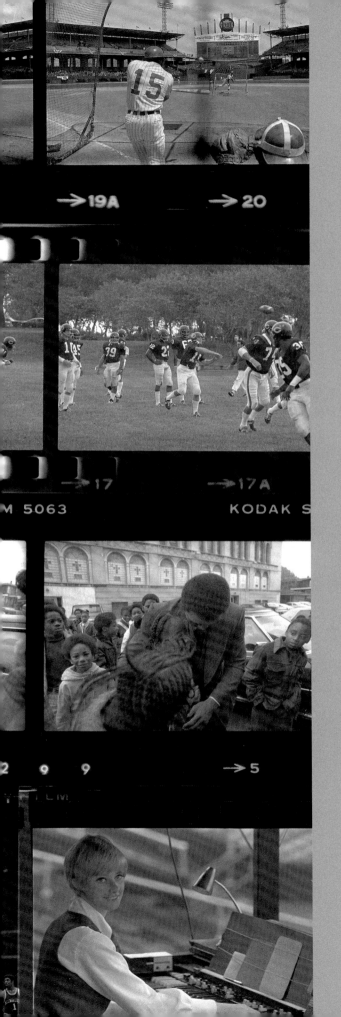

"I HAD ONLY ATTENDED ONE MAJOR LEAGUE BASEBALL GAME IN MY LIFE WHEN I GOT THE CALL TO PLAY FOR THE WHITE SOX. THE SOX HEARD ME PLAY AT A SPORTS LUNCHEON AND CALLED ME WHEN THEY NEEDED A NEW ORGANIST. THEY HEARD ME AND THOUGHT I WAS CAPABLE.

"THE DAY I SHOWED UP FOR MY JOB, I WAS HANDED A PIECE OF PAPER WITH THE PLAYERS' NAMES AND THE STATES WHERE THEY WERE FROM. THAT WAS IT. MY FIRST YEAR, 1970, WAS THE YEAR THE SOX HAD THEIR LOWEST ATTENDANCE—ABOUT 340,000 PEOPLE, SO IT WAS EASY FOR ME TO BREAK IN.

"I LOOSENED UP AS I MET FANS AND GOT MORE FAMILIAR WITH BASEBALL TERMINOLOGY. I WOULD USE BASEBALL WORDS TO ASSOCIATE WITH SONGS THAT I PLAYED. FOR WALKS, I WOULD PLAY, 'STROLLING THROUGH THE PARK ONE DAY,' OR 'STANDING ON THE CORNER, WATCHING ALL THE GIRLS GO BY.' THINGS WERE LAID BACK IN THOSE DAYS. IT WAS JUST THE PA MAN, ME AND THE GAME.

"MY FONDEST MEMORIES OF THE EARLY 1970S WERE OF THE PLAYERS. I BECAME A BIG FAN. I ESPECIALLY LIKED RICHIE ALLEN, BUT I NEVER REALLY GOT TO KNOW HIM. HE HAD A GREAT STANCE, AND HE WALKED AROUND WITH CONFIDENCE. HE WAS INDEPENDENT, AND HE DEFINED THE TEAM.

"BILL VEECK CHANGED EVERYTHING WHEN HE BOUGHT THE TEAM IN 1975. HE HAD ALL THESE ETHNIC DAYS, AND I HAD TO LEARN ALL THESE ANTHEMS. THAT WAS A STRUGGLE BECAUSE I PLAY BY EAR. I'D HAVE TO GET A RECORDING OR GET THE MUSIC.

"IT SEEMS LIKE EVERY FRIDAY NIGHT, WHEN BILL VEECK OWNED THE TEAM, BEER FIGHTS BROKE OUT. YOU WOULD SEE BEERS FLYING. PEOPLE WOULD JUST THROW BEERS AT EACH OTHER. I GUESS THEY WEREN'T SO EXPENSIVE THEN.

"NA-NA-NA-NA WAS NOT PLANNED. THE SONG, 'NA NA HEY HEY (KISS HIM GOODBYE),' WAS RELEASED BY STEAM IN 1969, AND I PLAYED IT FOR MANY YEARS BEFORE I GOT A RESPONSE. IN 1977, WE WERE IN THE MIDDLE OF A SERIES AGAINST KANSAS CITY, BOTH IN FIRST PLACE. PEOPLE JUST PICKED UP ON IT, AND THE SONG BECAME OUR ANTHEM. I STILL PLAY IT TODAY, AT THE RIGHT TIME WHEN THE SOX ARE AHEAD. USUALLY I PLAY IT WHEN THE OPPOSING TEAM CHANGES ITS PITCHER.

"DISCO DEMOLITION NIGHT . . . SURREAL. WHEN I LOOK BACK AT THE TAPE, I REALIZE PEOPLE WERE CHANTING 'DISCO SUCKS, DISCO SUCKS.' I JUST PICKED UP ON IT, PLAYING ALONG, THINKING THAT WAS THE SPIRIT OF THE NIGHT. THAT WAS BEFORE EVERYTHING GOT OUT OF HAND. AT ONE POINT THEY HAD ME PLAYING 'TAKE ME OUT TO THE BALL GAME.' WE TRIED TO PULL OUT ALL THE STOPS, BUT THERE WAS NO WAY TO CALM PEOPLE DOWN."

—NANCY FAUST, WHITE SOX ORGANIST

FROM TOP LEFT: WHITE SOX FIRST BASEMAN DICK ALLEN PHOTOS BY JOHN H. WHITE, BEARS WORKOUT PHOTOS BY HENRY HERR GILL, BOXER MUHAMMAD ALI PHOTO BY JAMES DEPREE, BULLS GAME PHOTOS BY JOE MARINO AND SOX ORGANIST NANCY FAUST PHOTO BY JOHN H. WHITE.

THE SEVENTIES

ERNIE'S 500TH. PHOTO BY HENRY HERR
GILL, MAY 13, 1970
CUBS FAITHFUL SHOWER APPLAUSE ON
ERNIE BANKS AFTER HIS 500TH HOMER
RUN. BANKS FINISHED HIS CAREER WITH
512 HOMERS.

A NEW LOOK.
BLACKHAWKS DEFENSEMAN KEITH MAGNUSON SHOWS OFF HIS PSYCHEDELIC APARTMENT IN SUBURBAN GLENVIEW ON
DECEMBER 7, 1973. MAGNUSON, WHO WAS NURSING AN INJURY, HELPED LEAD THE HAWKS' BACK LINE FOR A DECADE
STARTING IN 1969 AND SERVED AS HEAD COACH DURING THE EARLY 1980S. (PHOTO BY CHARLES KREJCSI.) LEFT:
BULLS FORWARD BOB LOVE PAUSES WITH HIS DAUGHTER, BASHA, AT HIS SUBURBAN PALATINE HOME ON APRIL 30,
1975. LOVE LED THE BULLS IN SCORING FOR SEVEN YEARS, AND ALMOST CARRIED THE TEAM TO THE NBA FINALS THAT
YEAR, BUT THE BULLS LOST THE CONFERENCE FINALS TO THE GOLDEN STATE WARRIORS IN SEVEN GAMES. (PHOTO
BY CARMEN REPORTO.)

THAT '70S SHOW.

FORMER BEARS STAR GEORGE BLANDA RETURNS TO CHICAGO TO TRY TO KICK A FOOTBALL ACROSS THE CHICAGO RIVER FOR A PUBLICITY STUNT ON JUNE 14, 1973. BUT THE RIVER WAS MORE THAN 100 YARDS WIDE AT THAT POINT, AND BLANDA PLOPPED EIGHT FOOTBALLS IN THE MIDDLE. "AT MIDSEASON, 18 YEARS AGO, I COULD HAVE DONE IT," SAID THE FUTURE HALL OF FAMER. (PHOTO BY JERRY TOMASELLI.) RIGHT: CUBS OUTFIELDER-FIRST BASEMAN JOE PEPITONE PEDDLES HIS WIGS AT A DRAKE HOTEL COCKTAIL PARTY TO INTRODUCE HIS NEW HAIRPIECE BUSINESS. PEPITONE SUPPLEMENTED HIS LONG SIDEBURNS WITH TWO WIGS, A FLOWING HAIRPIECE FOR SOCIAL OCCASIONS AND A "GAMER" FOR THE FIELD. (PHOTO BY EDMUND JARECKI.)

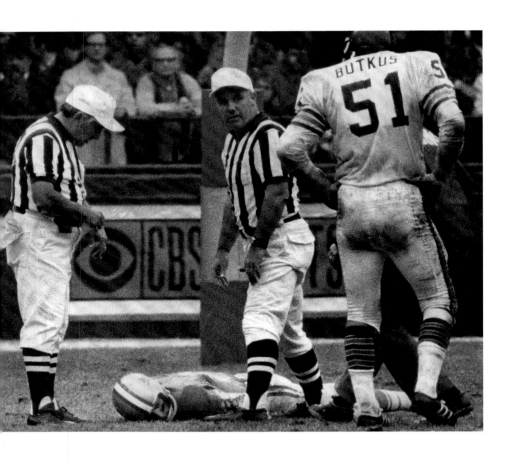

DEATH ON THE FIELD. PHOTO BY BOB LANGER, OCTOBER 24, 1971
BEARS LINEBACKER DICK BUTKUS LOOKS OVER THE STRICKEN CHUCK HUGHES AFTER
THE DETROIT LIONS WIDE RECEIVER COLLAPSED AND DIED ON THE FIELD AT TIGER STA-
DIUM IN DETROIT. BUTKUS, THE FIRST TO NOTICE HUGHES, QUICKLY CALLED THE LIONS
BENCH FOR HELP, BUT RESUSCITATION EFFORTS FAILED.

RIGHT: DEATH OFF THE FIELD. PHOTO BY PAUL SEQUEIRA, JUNE 19, 1970
TEAMMATES OF BRIAN PICCOLO, SERVING AS PALLBEARERS, MOVE SLOWLY FROM
CHRIST THE KING CATHOLIC CHURCH, CARRYING THE COFFIN OF THE FORMER BEARS
RUNNING BACK TO A WAITING HEARSE. FROM FRONT AT LEFT ARE ED O'BRADOVICH,
MIKE PYLE AND RALPH KUREK. FROM FRONT AT RIGHT ARE RANDY JACKSON, DICK
BUTKUS (OBSCURED) AND GALE SAYERS. PICCOLO, 26, DIED AFTER AN EIGHT-MONTH
BATTLE AGAINST CANCER. CONSIDERED TOO SMALL, HE PLAYED FOR THE TEAM FOR FOUR
SEASONS. SAID GEORGE HALAS, WHEN TOLD OF PICCOLO'S DEATH, "AH, HE WAS SUCH
A TOUGH ONE."

LONG SEASONS.
GOALIE TONY ESPOSITO THINKS ABOUT NEXT YEAR AFTER THE BLACKHAWKS BLEW A 2-0 SECOND-PERIOD LEAD
IN GAME 7 OF THE STANLEY CUP FINALS TO LOSE TO THE MONTREAL CANADIANS ON MAY 18, 1971. (PHOTO BY
LARRY GRAFF.) RIGHT: THE CUBS HEAD TO THE DRESSING ROOM AT THE END OF THE 1972 SEASON ON OCTO-
BER 4. THE TEAM FINISHED THE YEAR 85-70, THEIR LAST WINNING SEASON UNTIL 1984, WHEN THEY WON THE
NATIONAL LEAGUE EAST DIVISION. (PHOTO BY BOB LANGER.)

MOTTA'S MEN.
BULLS COACH DICK MOTTA TAKES HIS TEAM THROUGH A WORKOUT ON MARCH 30, 1970, TO PREPARE FOR THE PLAYOFFS. THE 1969-70 TEAM WAS THE HIGHEST-SCORING BULLS TEAM IN HISTORY, BUT THE BULLS LOST THE WESTERN DIVISION SEMIFINALS 4 GAMES TO 1 TO THE ATLANTA HAWKS. MOTTA COACHED THE TEAM FOR EIGHT SEASONS. (PHOTO BY BOB LANGER.) RIGHT: LAKERS CENTER WILT CHAMBERLAIN DUNKS DURING THE BULLS PLAYOFF GAME AGAINST THE LAKERS ON APRIL 2, 1972. THE BULLS COULDN'T SEEM TO GET PAST CHAMBERLAIN OR KAREEM ABDUL-JABBAR DURING THE EARLY 1970S PLAYOFFS. (PHOTO BY FRED STEIN.)

CHEAP SEATS.
AN OVERHEAD VIEW OF A RECORD CROWD OF 19,690, WHICH JAMMED CHICAGO STADIUM TO SEE THE BULLS
BEAT THE 76ERS ON DECEMBER 14, 1976. (PHOTO BY BOB LANGER.) TOP RIGHT: CENTER TOM BOERWINKLE
SHOWS HIS HOOK ON FEBRUARY 1, 1970. BOERWINKLE PLAYED 10 YEARS WITH THE BULLS. ONLY MICHAEL
JORDAN AND SCOTTIE PIPPEN PLAYED MORE. (PHOTO BY JACK LENAHAN.) RIGHT: CHET WALKER, A PERENNIAL
ALL-STAR WITH THE BULLS, DRIVES TO THE BASKET ON JANUARY 25, 1975. (PHOTO BY BOB LANGER.)

DEFENSE WAS KEY.
JERRY SLOAN GRABS A REBOUND ON DECEMBER 4. 1971. SLOAN, THE TEAM'S TOUGHEST DEFENDER, WAS ACQUIRED IN THE BULLS' FIRST EXPANSION DRAFT. (PHOTO BY BOB LANGER.) RIGHT: NORM VAN LIER DRIVES AROUND THE NEW YORK KNICKS' WALT FRAZIER ON FEBRUARY 12, 1975. VAN LIER HELPED LEAD THE BULLS FOR SEVEN YEARS DURING THE 1970S. (PHOTO BY JACK LENAHAN.)

ROLLER DERBY REVIVAL. PHOTOS BY CHUCK KIRMAN, SEPTEMBER 15, 1972
THE MIDWEST PIONEERS TAKE ON THE LOS ANGELES THUNDERBIRDS AT A ROCKIN'
COMISKEY PARK. AN ANNOUNCED CROWD OF 50,118 FANS—MORE PEOPLE THAN HAD
WATCHED A WHITE SOX GAME IN 17 YEARS—CAME TO SEE THE BLOCKERS AND JAM-
MERS SQUARE OFF. ANOTHER 15,000 WERE REPORTEDLY TURNED AWAY. THE SPORT,
STARTED IN 1935 AT THE CHICAGO COLISEUM, FLOURISHED IN THE DECADE AFTER
WORLD WAR II, BUT IT FELL VICTIM TO OVEREXPOSURE ON TV.

Santa Fe finish line. Photo by Larry Graff, July 27, 1977
Stock cars head down the straightaway at the Santa Fe Speedway in suburban Willow Springs. In the 1940s and 1950s, car races were held at Soldier Field, O'Hare Stadium, Raceway Park and Santa Fe. The speedway opened in 1895—for horse racing. A half-mile clay track was built for car racing in the early 1950s. The track also hosted races for motorcycles and midget cars, as well as demolition derbies. It was replaced by a housing development in the 1990s.

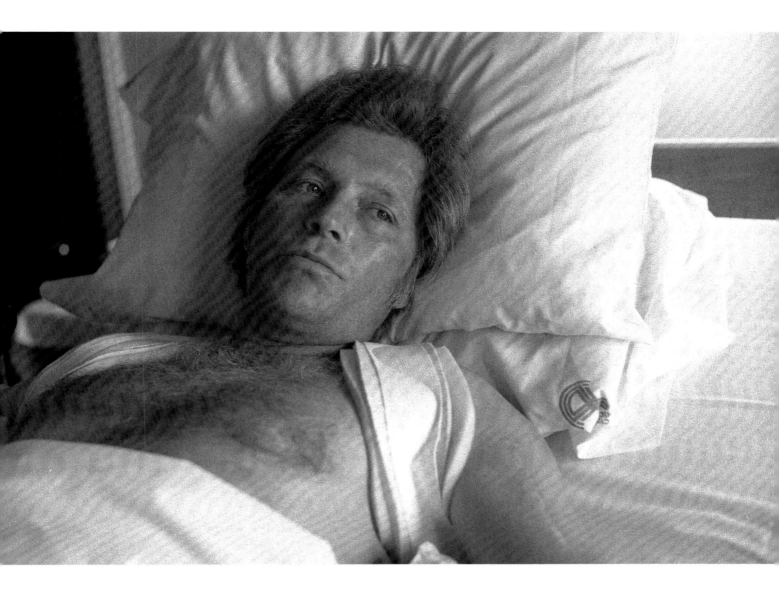

THE REAL SHARK.

DAREDEVIL EVEL KNIEVEL STARES OUT THE WINDOW OF A MICHAEL REESE HOSPITAL ROOM ON FEBRUARY 1, 1977, AFTER SUFFERING MULTIPLE FRACTURES IN PRACTICE. KNIEVEL WAS SUPPOSED TO JUMP HIS MOTOR-CYCLE OVER A POOL OF 13 MAN-EATING SHARKS AT THE INTERNATIONAL AMPHITHEATER BEFORE A NATIONAL TV AUDIENCE, BUT HE SLAMMED INTO A RETAINING WALL HOURS BEFORE THE REAL JUMP. (PHOTO BY MARTHA HARTNETT.) LEFT: ABOUT 3,000 PEOPLE SHOWED UP FOR THE JANUARY 31 EVENT AT THE AMPHITHEATER. THEY WERE OFFERED REFUNDS. (PHOTO BY EDMUND JARECKI.)

WOMEN IN WAITING.

FOURTEEN-YEAR-OLD ANDREA JAEGER, OF SUBURBAN LINCOLNSHIRE, STRUMS HER TENNIS RACQUET ON NO-
VEMBER 28, 1979, AFTER THE STEVENSON HIGH SCHOOL FRESHMAN WAS RANKED NUMBER 1 IN THE NATION IN
THE 18-AND-UNDER AGE GROUP. JAEGER TURNED PRO THAT YEAR AND SOON ROSE TO NUMBER 2 IN THE WORLD.
HER CAREER ENDED AFTER SHE SUFFERED A SHOULDER INJURY FIVE YEARS LATER. (PHOTO BY BOB LANGER.)
RIGHT: BILLY JEAN KING FINISHES SECOND IN THE VIRGINIA SLIMS TENNIS TOURNEY ON MARCH 11, 1973,
AT THE LAKE SHORE RACQUET CLUB. LATER THAT YEAR, KING WON THE BATTLE-OF-THE-SEXES MATCH AGAINST
BOBBY RIGGS AND FOUNDED THE WOMEN'S TENNIS ASSOCIATION. (PHOTO BY FRED STEIN.)

NEW MANAGEMENT.
ABOVE: WHITE SOX FAN BOB SKREZYNA BITES HIS NAILS AT THE FIRST GAME OF THE 1978 SEASON ON
APRIL 7. (PHOTO BY KEVIN HORAN.) LEFT: BILL VEECK MAKES HIS GRAND REAPPEARANCE AT SOX PARK
ON OPENING DAY OF THE 1976 SEASON, MARCHING FROM CENTER FIELD TO HOME. TO MARK THE BICEN-
TENNIAL, VEECK CALLED OUT THE FIFE AND DRUM CORP. PEG-LEGGED VEECK (RIGHT) PLAYED THE FIFE,
SOX MANAGER PAUL RICHARDS HOISTED THE FLAG AND RUDIE SCHAFFER PLAYED THE DRUM. A CROWD OF
40,000 HAILED THE CONQUERING HEROES ON APRIL 9. (PHOTO BY BOB LANGER.)

COMISKEY LIFE.
FANS PILE UP SOFT DRINK CUPS IWO JIMA-STYLE IN MAY 1970. (PHOTO BY DON BIERMAN.) LEFT: A FIGHT BREAKS OUT, ONE OF MANY, ON OPENING DAY IN 1975. POLICE AND SECURITY MEN FORCE A BRAWLER OVER THE OUTFIELD WALL AS A GUARD SLUGS HIM IN THE FACE ON APRIL 15. (PHOTO BY FRED STEIN.)

TRICK PITCH. PHOTOS BY BOB LANGER.
RIGHT: CUBS PITCHER BRUCE SUTTER TAKES A BREAK FROM THE HEAT IN THE DUGOUT ON JULY 23, 1979, DURING
HIS CY YOUNG AWARD SEASON. ABOVE: SUTTER LEARNED HIS TRADEMARK PITCH, THE SPLIT-FINGER FASTBALL,
AFTER ARM SURGERY THREATENED HIS CAREER. HE WAS THE CUBS CLOSER FROM 1976 TO 1980.

AWAY FROM THE MADDING CROWD. PHOTOS BY JOHN H. WHITE, JULY 22, 1978
MUHAMMAD ALI TRAINS AT HIS DEER LAKE, PENNSYLVANIA, CAMP FOR A FIGHT AGAINST LEON SPINKS. ALI
HAD LOST THE TITLE TO SPINKS IN FEBRUARY 1978, BUT DEFEATED HIM FIVE MONTHS LATER. PHOTOGRAPHER
WHITE, ALI'S FRIEND, ACCOMPANIED HIM TO THE SECLUDED, RUSTIC TRAINING CAMP SEVERAL TIMES.

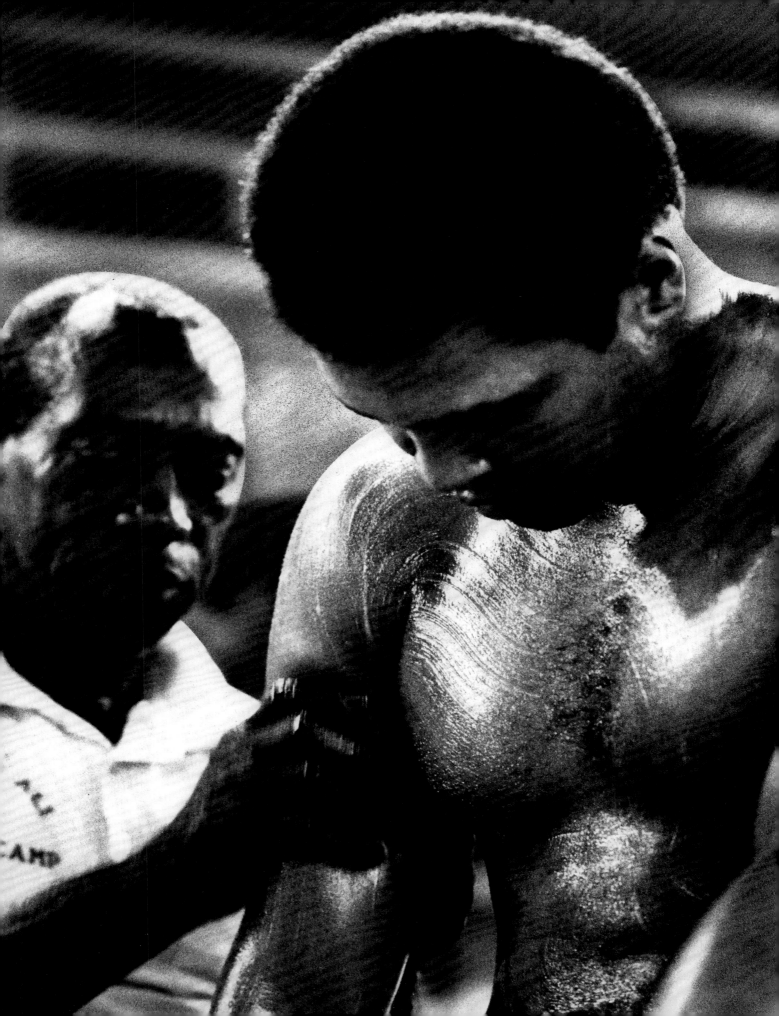

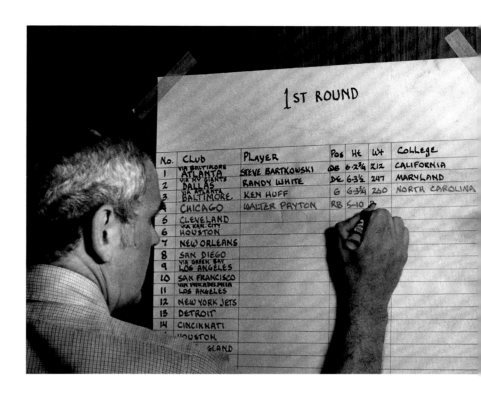

1ST ROUND

No.	Club	Player	Pos	Ht	Wt	College
1	ATLANTA (VIA BALTIMORE)	STEVE BARTKOWSKI	QB	6-2¾	212	CALIFORNIA
2	DALLAS (VIA NY GIANTS)	RANDY WHITE	DE	6-3½	247	MARYLAND
3	BALTIMORE (VIA ATLANTA)	KEN HUFF	G	6-3¾	260	NORTH CAROLINA
4	CHICAGO	WALTER PAYTON	RB	5-10		
6	CLEVELAND					
6	HOUSTON (VIA KAN. CITY)					
7	NEW ORLEANS					
8	SAN DIEGO					
9	LOS ANGELES (VIA GREEN BAY)					
10	SAN FRANCISCO					
11	LOS ANGELES (VIA PHILADELPHIA)					
12	NEW YORK JETS					
13	DETROIT					
14	CINCINNATI					
	HOUSTON					
	GLAND					

SWEETEST DAY.
THE NAME OF WALTER PAYTON, OF JACKSON STATE UNIVERSITY, IS PENCILED ONTO
THE LIST OF FIRST-ROUND DRAFTEES JANUARY 28, 1975, AT THE LASALLE HOTEL BY
BILL MCGRANE, ASSISTANT TO BEARS GENERAL MANAGER JIM FINKS. (PHOTO BY HEN-
RY HERR GILL.) LEFT: PAYTON FINDS RUNNING ROOM AFTER TAKING A HANDOFF FROM
QUARTERBACK BOB AVELLINI AT CANDLESTICK PARK IN SAN FRANCISCO ON SEPTEM-
BER 19, 1976. THE PHOTO WAS TAKEN BY FRED STEIN FROM THE PRESS BOX AS PART
OF A CHICAGO DAILY NEWS FEATURE CALLED PRO PHOTO FOOTBALL—WHICH SHOWED
KEY PLAYS IN SEQUENCE. THE PICTURE, CALLED "RING AROUND THE RUNNER," WON
THE PRO FOOTBALL HALL OF FAME PHOTO CONTEST IN 1976, AND HUNG—AT LEAST
ACCORDING TO LORE—BEHIND THE DESK OF GEORGE HALAS.

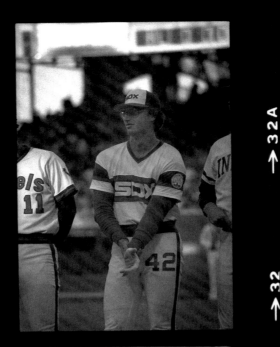
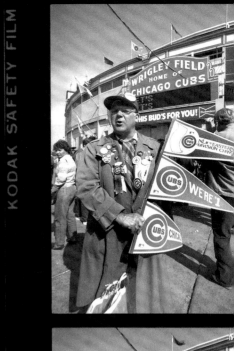

"In 1983, the Bears were 8-8. We won five of our last six games and showed that we were getting better. We had a big draft that year that included Willie Gault, Jimbo Covert and Richard Dent. Walter Payton had been with the Bears since 1975, so by 1984 we sensed we had a chance to win the NFL title. We were 6-3 that year when I blew my kidney out against the Los Angeles Raiders. We finished with a 10-6 record and won the division. Steve Fuller led us to victory in the first round of the playoffs, but we lost the NFC Championship game to the San Francisco 49ers. We felt that we should have won the title.

"Coming into training camp in 1985, we knew that we had a really good football team. Also, we had picked up Wilber Marshall in 1984. Mark Bortz and Otis Wilson were already with the Bears, so the majority of our defense was in place for the '85 season. We won the opener, but surprisingly we didn't play well defensively in the early part of the season. The key game for us was Week 3, in Minnesota. Coach Mike Ditka said that I wasn't going to play because I had missed practice for three days. So there I was, watching the game, and we were getting beaten. I finally bugged Ditka enough to get him to put me in the game, and we won.

"Mike just wanted to be in control of everything. Even though there were members of the defense who didn't practice each week, Ditka wouldn't let me play if I missed just one day of practice. We had the best players that year and didn't need a lot of fancy plays.

"After Minnesota, we got on a roll, winning nine in a row until Miami beat us for our only loss of the season. I don't think that we should have lost that game. I had missed two days of practice because of a sprained ankle, so Mike said Steve Fuller would be the quarterback. Miami had the worst rush defense in the league, so Walter should have had 300 yards that night. But Miami scored quickly, and Ditka decided to start throwing the ball. I didn't get in that game until there were six minutes to go. The loss didn't bother Ditka because we were already in the playoffs and had already won the division with a month to play.

"After Miami, we swept through the rest of the season, including the Super Bowl. For the next five years, we had the best players and best team in the NFL. We just never brought it home again."

—Jim McMahon, former Chicago Bears quarterback

THE EIGHTIES

JUST FOR KICKS. PHOTO BY TOM CRUZE, AUGUST 30, 1981
CHICAGO STING FORWARD KARL-HEINZ GRANITZA LEAPS INTO
THE ARMS OF TEAMMATE DEREK SPALDING AFTER SPALDING'S
PENALTY KICK TIED THE QUARTERFINAL GAME BETWEEN THE
STING AND THE SEATTLE SOUNDERS AT WRIGLEY FIELD. PLAY-
ING ONE MAN SHORT, THE STING SCORED THREE SECOND-HALF
GOALS TO BEAT THE SOUNDERS 3-2 AND ADVANCE TO THE
NORTH AMERICAN SOCCER LEAGUE SEMIFINALS. THE STING
WENT ON TO WIN THE SEMIFINALS AND THE SOCCER BOWL, AND
BRING HOME CHICAGO'S FIRST PRO SPORTS CHAMPIONSHIP IN
18 YEARS.

DePaul loses—again. Photos by Dom Najolia, March 14, 1981
DePaul guard Clyde Bradshaw is stunned after John Smith of St. Joseph's
College makes a layup to eliminate DePaul in the NCAA Regionals. It was the
second year in a row that top-seeded DePaul lost in the early rounds of the
tournament. Right: Coach Ray Meyer returns from Dayton, Ohio, with guard
Skip Dillard, who missed a key free throw with 12 seconds left. "Sometimes
even the best miss," Meyer said.

A LOOK AT TENNIS.
A DOUBLE EXPOSURE SHOWS TENNIS FANS TRYING TO KEEP UP WITH THE SEMIFINAL MATCH OF THE AVON TENNIS CHAMPIONSHIPS AT THE INTERNATIONAL AMPHITHEATRE ON JANUARY 26, 1980. THE MATCH WAS BETWEEN CHRIS EVERT LLOYD AND WENDY TURNBULL. (PHOTO BY BOB LANGER.) RIGHT: JOHN MCENROE TORTURED HIMSELF IN A JANUARY 1982 HORIZON CHALLENGE MATCH IN SUBURBAN ROSEMONT. MCENROE, THE WORLD'S TOP-RANKED PLAYER AT THE TIME, LOST THE CHAMPIONSHIP TO JIMMY CONNORS. (PHOTO BY TOM CRUZE.)

AND NOW, IN CENTER FIELD . . . .
ROOKIE SOX OUTFIELDER JOHN CANGELOSI RUNS OUT OF ROOM WHILE TRACKING DOWN A TRIPLE HIT BY
NEW YORK YANKEE DON MATTINGLY ON JULY 5, 1986. THE PHOTO WAS NAMED BEST OF THE YEAR BY
THE NATIONAL BASEBALL HALL OF FAME. (PHOTO BY TOM CRUZE.) LEFT: HARRY CARAY BROADCASTS HIS
FINAL GAME AT COMISKEY PARK ON OCTOBER 4, 1981. CARAY WAS THE VOICE OF THE WHITE SOX FROM
1971 TO 1981, PAIRING WITH JIMMY PIERSALL FOR SEVERAL SEASONS. (PHOTO BY BARRY JARVINEN.)

HEY, HEY—GOODBYE.
AS MANY AS 50,000 WHITE SOX FANS JAMMED THE DALEY CENTER PLAZA ON OCTOBER 3, 1983, TO SEND THEIR
TEAM TO THE AMERICAN LEAGUE PLAYOFFS IN BALTIMORE. THE SOX FINISHED THE SEASON WITH A 99-63 RECORD,
WINNING THE AMERICAN LEAGUE WEST TITLE BY 20 GAMES. (PHOTO BY PHIL VELASQUEZ.) RIGHT: CATCHER CARL-
TON FISK GETS A HUG FROM HIS DAUGHTER, CARLYN, ON OCTOBER 8, AFTER THE SOX WERE ELIMINATED FROM THE
PLAYOFF BY THE ORIOLES. AFTER WINNING THE FIRST GAME OF THE SERIES, THE SOX COULD ONLY MANAGE ONE
RUN IN THE FINAL THREE GAMES. (PHOTO BY JOHN KEATING.)

ON ICE SINCE 1945. PHOTOS BY PHIL VELASQUEZ, SEPTEMBER 24, 1984
RYNE SANDBERG (ABOVE) AND RICK SUTCLIFFE (RIGHT) CELEBRATE THE CUBS FIRST CHAMPIONSHIP IN 39
YEARS, AFTER THEY BEAT THE PITTSBURGH PIRATES TO CLINCH THE NATIONAL LEAGUE EAST CROWN. SUT-
CLIFFE WON THE CY YOUNG AWARD; SANDBERG WON THE MOST VALUABLE PLAYER.

TURN OUT THE LIGHTS.
LEFT: CUBS OUTFIELDER KEITH MORELAND (6) AND SHORTSTOP LARRY BOWA HIGH-FIVE AFTER THE CUBS WON GAME 1 OF THE NATIONAL LEAGUE CHAMPIONSHIP SERIES 13-0 AGAINST THE SAN DIEGO PADRES ON OCTOBER 2, 1984. (PHOTO BY BOB RINGHAM.) ABOVE: FIVE DAYS LATER, CUBS FANS WATCH THEIR WORLD SERIES DREAMS SLIP AWAY ON TV AS THE PADRES SCORE SIX LATE-INNING RUNS TO WIN THE NATIONAL LEAGUE PENNANT AND ADVANCE TO THE WORLD SERIES. THESE FANS WERE AT MURPHY'S BLEACHERS, ACROSS FROM WRIGLEY FIELD. (PHOTOS BY AL PODGORSKI.)

SECOND-BALCONY CROWD. PHOTOS BY BOB LANGER.
BLACKHAWKS FANS WATCH THE SEASON OPENER AGAINST TORONTO AT THE CHICAGO STADIUM ON OCTOBER 6, 1982. THE HAWKS FINISHED IN FIRST PLACE FOUR TIMES DURING THE 1980S, AND MADE IT TO THE PLAY-OFFS EVERY YEAR THAT DECADE. RIGHT: TEAMMATES RUSH TO CONGRATULATE GOALIE TONY ESPOSITO AFTER THE HAWKS STUNNED THE MINNESOTA NORTH STARS AND ELIMINATED THEM FROM THE PLAYOFFS ON APRIL 11, 1982. THE HAWKS WENT ON TO BEAT THE ST. LOUIS BLUES, BUT ENDED THE SEASON LOSING TO THE VANCOUVER CANUCKS.

A SEASON TO SAVOR.
THE 1985 CHICAGO BEARS—WHICH FINISHED 15-1, WON TWO PLAYOFF GAMES BY SHUTOUTS AND TOOK THE SUPER BOWL CROWN—
WAS A TEAM CHOCK FULL OF PERSONALITY. TOP ROW FROM LEFT: DEFENSIVE COORDINATOR BUDDY RYAN (PHOTO BY BOB RINGHAM.),
DEFENSIVE BACK GARY FENCIK (PHOTO BY AL PODGORSKI.), DEFENSIVE LINEMAN/RUNNING BACK WILLIAM "REFRIGERATOR" PERRY
WITH COMEDIAN/BEARS FAN BOB HOPE (PHOTO BY AMANDA ALCOCK.) AND QUARTERBACK JIM MCMAHON. (PHOTO BY TOM CRUZE.)

SECOND ROW: THE GREAT WALTER PAYTON (PHOTO BY BOB RINGHAM.), LINEBACKER MIKE SINGLETARY (PHOTO BY BOB RINGHAM.), DEFENSIVE LINEMAN DAN HAMPTON (PHOTO BY JOHN H. WHITE.) AND RUNNING BACK MATT SUHEY. (PHOTO BY TOM CRUZE.) BOTTOM ROW: KICKER KEVIN BUTLER (PHOTO BY TOM CRUZE.), WIDE RECEIVER WILLIE GAULT WITH BALLERINA MARIA TEREZIA BALOGH (PHOTO BY JACK LENAHAN.), LINEBACKER OTIS WILSON (PHOTO BY AL PODGORSKI.) AND A DIEHARD FAN. (PHOTO BY JOHN H. WHITE.)

SUPER MEN. JANUARY 26, 1986
BEARS COACH MIKE DITKA IS CARRIED OFF THE FIELD BY DEFENSIVE LINEMEN WILLIAM PERRY (FOREGROUND)
AND STEVE MCMICHAEL AFTER THE BEARS DEFEATED THE NEW ENGLAND PATRIOTS 46-10 IN SUPER BOWL XX.
(PHOTO BY PHIL VELASQUEZ.) LEFT: ROWDY FANS FILL THE RUSH STREET NEIGHBORHOOD IN CELEBRATION.
(PHOTO BY ROBERT REEDER.)

BEARS WIN! WE THINK. DECEMBER 31, 1988
IT WAS CONSIDERED THE BEST GAME NOBODY SAW. A DENSE FOG
ROLLED INTO SOLDIER FIELD OFF THE SHORE OF LAKE MICHIGAN
DURING THE SECOND QUARTER OF THE PLAYOFF GAME BETWEEN THE
BEARS AND PHILADELPHIA EAGLES. AFTER THE FOG, ONLY TWO FIELD
GOALS WERE SCORED—ONE FOR EACH TEAM. (PHOTO BY TOM CRUZE.)
RIGHT: BEARS LINEBACKER MIKE SINGLETARY HUGS EAGLES LINE-
MAN REGGIE WHITE AND BEARS DEFENSIVE BACK DAVE DUERSON
AFTER THE GAME. THE BEARS LOST THE CONFERENCE CHAMPIONSHIP
TO THE 49ERS THE NEXT WEEK. (PHOTO BY PHIL VELASQUEZ.)

MORNING HAS BROKEN. PHOTO BY TOM CRUZE, JULY 31, 1988
TRIATHLETES PERFORM THEIR EARLY-MORNING WARM-UP AT OAK STREET BEACH PRIOR TO THE START OF
THE CHICAGO BUD LIGHT TRIATHLON. THE CITY'S FIRST MAJOR TRIATHLON WAS HELD IN 1983, WITH 760
COMPETITORS. BY 1988, 3,000 ATHLETES WERE RUNNING, BIKING AND SWIMMING IN THE EVENT.

So much promise. Photo by John H. White, November 21, 1984
Students at Simeon Vocational High School place Ben Wilson's graduation photo on his gown at a memorial. Wilson, considered one of the best high school basketball players in the nation, was shot during a robbery attempt while on his lunch break near the school. He died the next day—at age 17. He was buried in his high school basketball uniform.

A RUNNER'S-EYE VIEW. OCTOBER 21, 1984
SUN-TIMES PHOTOGRAPHER AL PODGORSKI WAS ONE OF NEARLY 8,000 RUNNERS AT THE STARTING LINE OF THE 1984
CHICAGO MARATHON. PODGORSKI RAN THE ENTIRE 26.2 MILES CARRYING A 35-MILLIMETER CAMERA. HE TOOK ALONG
EIGHT ROLLS OF FILM—WHICH HE STORED IN HIS SOCKS. "IT WAS COLD AND RAINY, BUT PEOPLE LINED THE NEIGHBOR-
HOODS CHEERING US ON," HE RECALLS. GREAT BRITAIN'S STEVE JONES SET A WORLD RECORD IN THE RACE, FINISHING
IN 2 HOURS, 8 MINUTES AND 5 SECONDS, FAR AHEAD OF THE RUNNER WITH A CAMERA.

WALKING ON AIR. PHOTO BY TOM CRUZE, FEBRUARY 6, 1988

MICHAEL JORDAN TAKES OFF AT THE FREE-THROW LINE TO CAPTURE THE SLAM DUNK CHAMPIONSHIP PRIOR TO THE NBA ALL-STAR GAME AT THE CHICAGO STADIUM. ALL-STAR WEEKEND WAS A CORONATION OF SORTS FOR JORDAN AS THE KING OF BASKETBALL. AFTER WINNING HIS SECOND CONSECUTIVE SLAM DUNK EVENT, HE WAS NAMED MOST VALUABLE PLAYER IN THE ALL-STAR GAME, SCORING 40 POINTS. EVEN JORDAN WAS IMPRESSED. "LIKE A SCRIPT," HE SAID.

HIDE-YOUR-FACE WIN.
PHOTO BY BOB RINGHAM, MAY 19, 1989
COACH DOUG COLLINS IS OVERCOME WITH
EMOTION AS THE BULLS BEAT THE NEW YORK
KNICKS AT CHICAGO STADIUM TO ADVANCE—
FOR THE FIRST TIME IN 14 YEARS—TO THE
EASTERN CONFERENCE FINALS. THE BULLS
LOST TO THE DETROIT PISTONS 4 GAMES TO
2 IN THE CONFERENCE FINALS. COLLINS WAS
FIRED AT THE END OF THE SEASON.

SWITCHEROO.
PHOTO BY AL PODGORSKI,
AUGUST 8, 1988
HARRY GROSSMAN, A CUBS
FAN SINCE 1906, TURNS ON
540 LIGHTS ATOP WRIGLEY
FIELD BEFORE THE CUBS
PLAYED THEIR FIRST NIGHT
GAME. HE WAS HELPED BY
BALLGIRL MARY ELLEN KAPP.

FUN AND FROLIC AT WRIGLEY.
OPENING NIGHT FOR THE CUBS: THE VIEW OF THE LIGHT-BATHED STADIUM FROM THE WRIGLEY FIELD SCOREBOARD. (PHOTO BY TOM CRUZE.) CUBS PITCHERS GREG MADDUX (RIGHT) AND LES LANCASTER SKID ON THE TARP AFTER THE FIRST WRIGLEY FIELD NIGHT GAME WAS HALTED BY RAIN IN THE FOURTH INNING. WATCHING ARE TEAMMATES AL NIPPER (FAR LEFT) AND JODY DAVIS. (PHOTO BY AL PODGORSKI.) RIGHT: OUTFIELDER ANDRE DAWSON GETS HANDSHAKES AFTER HITTING A GRAND SLAM ON JUNE 1, 1987. DAWSON WAS NAMED THE NATIONAL LEAGUE'S MOST VALUABLE PLAYER THAT YEAR, HIS FIRST WITH THE CUBS. HE HELPED LEAD THE TEAM TO THE EAST DIVISION CHAMPIONSHIP IN 1989. (PHOTO BY PHIL VELASQUEZ.)

KODAK PPB 5113

KODAK PPB 5113

"AFTER FINISHING MY PLAYING CAREER IN THE LATE '70S, I CAME BACK TO CHICAGO JUST ONE YEAR BEFORE THE BULLS WON THEIR FIRST CHAMPIONSHIP IN 1991, AND I STARTED BROADCASTING. I WAS GIVEN A JOB TO OFFER ANALYSIS DURING HALFTIME AND AT THE END OF BULLS GAMES.

"THERE WAS EXCITEMENT THROUGHOUT CHICAGO DURING THE 1990S SINCE THE CITY WAS STARVED FOR A CHAMPIONSHIP, OR JUST A WINNER. I WAS HAPPY TO BE BACK. THE BULLS HAD WORKED HARD IN THE 1970S TO ESTABLISH A PROFESSIONAL FRANCHISE. WE HAD A GOOD TEAM THEN, AND THE TEAMS IN THE '90S WERE THE FRUIT COMING TO BEAR.

"I WAS JUST AS THRILLED AS ANYONE TO BE A PART OF THE CHAMPIONSHIP YEARS. I FELT THAT I HAD PERFORMED TWO ROLES: I HAD SERVED AS A PLAYER FOR SEVEN YEARS TO ESTABLISH THE TEAM, AND I HAD SERVED AS A BROADCASTER, CRITIQUING THE TEAM. KIDS DIDN'T KNOW THAT I HAD PLAYED FOR THE BULLS, BUT THEY RESPECTED ME AS A BROADCASTER.

"NEEDLESS TO SAY, IT WAS A THRILL TO WATCH MICHAEL JORDAN, THE GREATEST BASKETBALL PLAYER IN THE WORLD, PLAY IN OUR TOWN. SIX CHAMPIONSHIPS GAVE NOTORIETY TO THE CITY. CHICAGO HAD NEVER EXPERIENCED THAT KIND OF SUCCESS WITH ITS SPORTS TEAMS, AND THERE WAS GREAT EXCITEMENT SURROUNDING IT. CHICAGO DEVELOPED A REPUTATION FOR WINNING AND A REPUTATION FOR ENJOYING IT, TOO.

"CHICAGO STADIUM WAS PROBABLY THE NOISIEST PLACE TO BE, AND THE SOUND THAT SURROUNDED THE WINNING WAS UNBELIEVABLE. WE HAD SOME GREAT TEAMS IN THE '70S, TEAMS THAT MADE THE STADIUM ROCK AND ROLL. WE MADE SEVERAL RUNS IN THE FIRST PART OF THE DECADE, AND MADE A RUN IN THE LATE '70S WITH ARTIS GILMORE AS THE TEAM'S CENTER. I KNEW THE RUSH OF BEING HERE. I STILL REMEMBER THAT THE STADIUM WOULD ACTUALLY SHAKE WHEN WE CAME UP THE STAIRS DURING THE YEARS I PLAYED FOR THE BULLS. IT WAS ALMOST THE SAME TWO DECADES LATER.

"BUT SOMETHING WAS DIFFERENT.

"IN THE 1970S, THE STADIUM WAS FILLED WITH LOYAL, GOODHEARTED, WILD, CRAZY FANS WHO LIKED TO GET SEATS UP CLOSE TO THE ACTION. THESE EVERYDAY FANS WERE EVERYDAY PEOPLE. TWO DECADES LATER, THE FAN BASE WAS NOT THE SAME. BY 1990, THE STADIUM BEGAN TO BE FILLED WITH A CORPORATE CROWD. THESE WERE LOYAL, GOOD FANS, TOO, BUT THEY ARE QUIETER THAN THE CROWDS THAT CHEERED ON ME AND MY TEAMMATES. SOME OF THE EXCITEMENT WE FELT IN THE '70S WAS MISSING. IT WAS ONLY A SLIGHT DIFFERENCE, BUT I COULD FEEL IT."

—NORM VAN LIER, CHICAGO BULLS ANNOUNCER AND FORMER BULLS GUARD

FROM TOP LEFT: MICHAEL JORDAN PHOTOS BY TOM CRUZE, BULLS CELEBRATION PHOTOS BY TOM CRUZE, ANTHEM VIRTUOSO WAYNE MESSMER PHOTOS BY BOB RINGHAM, SAMMY SOSA AND FRANK THOMAS PHOTOS BY PHIL VELASQUEZ AND BEARS LINEBACKER MIKE SINGLETARY PHOTOS BY TOM CRUZE.

THE NINETIES...
TO TODAY

THE FINAL SEASON.
PHOTO BY TOM CRUZE.
WHITE SOX COACH BARRY
FOOTE WATCHES THE SOX
PLAY DURING THEIR FINAL
SEASON AT COMISKEY PARK
AS A NEW PARK RISES IN THE
BACKGROUND IN 1990. MORE
THAN 6,000 MAJOR LEAGUE
GAMES OVER 81 SEASONS
WERE PLAYED IN THE OLD
PARK, WHICH WAS BUILT IN
1910 FOR $750,000. THE
PARK WAS ALSO HOME TO THE
EAST-WEST NEGRO LEAGUE
ALL-STAR GAME AND FOOT-
BALL'S CHICAGO CARDINALS.
CONSTRUCTION OF THE $167-
MILLION NEW STADIUM START-
ED IN 1989. IT OPENED ON
APRIL 18, 1991.

THE NATURALS. JULY 11, 1990

BEFORE LEAVING OLD COMISKEY, THE SOX HELD THE FIRST TURN-BACK-THE-CLOCK DAY, DONNING 1917 UNI-FORMS IN HONOR OF THE ONLY COMISKEY PARK TEAM TO WIN THE WORLD SERIES. PHOTOGRAPHER TOM CRUZE CAME DECKED OUT IN A PURPLE, PLAID SUIT, BOW TIE, SPATS AND STRAW HAT. HE SHOT THE GAME USING A VINTAGE SPEED GRAPHIC CAMERA THAT PRODUCED THESE 4-BY-5-INCH NEGATIVES. ABOVE: SHORTSTOP OZZIE GUILLEN, WHO LOVED THE FLANNELS AND SUGGESTED PLAYING IN THEM THE REST OF THE SEASON. TOP RIGHT: PITCHERS BARRY JONES (LEFT) AND SCOTT RADINSKY. RIGHT: PITCHER WAYNE EDWARDS.

TEARING UP THE PLACE. PHOTOS BY TOM CRUZE.
LEFT: COMISKEY PARK IS DEMOLISHED DURING THE 1991 BASEBALL
SEASON. TWO YEARS LATER, THE SOX WON THE AMERICAN LEAGUE
WEST DIVISION CHAMPIONSHIP. ABOVE: BO JACKSON CELEBRATES
THE TEAM'S FIRST CROWN IN A DECADE AFTER THE CLINCHER ON
SEPTEMBER 27, 1993, IN WHICH HE HIT A THREE-RUN HOMER. THE
SOX LOST THE AMERICAN LEAGUE CHAMPIONSHIP SERIES TO THE
TORONTO BLUE JAYS 4 GAMES TO 2.

GAME ENDER. PHOTO BY TOM CRUZE, JUNE 6, 1995
BLACKHAWKS GOALIE ED BELFOUR DROPS TO THE ICE AFTER ALLOWING A GOAL IN THE SECOND OVERTIME
OF THE WESTERN CONFERENCE FINAL SERIES AGAINST THE DETROIT RED WINGS. THE HAWKS LOST TO THE
WINGS 4 GAMES TO 1. BELFOUR PLAYED MASTERFULLY THROUGH MUCH OF THE EARLY '90S, TAKING THE
TEAM TO THE STANLEY CUP FINALS ONCE—BUT FALLING TO THE PITTSBURGH PENGUINS IN 1992.

Damaged goods. Photo by Tom Cruze, February 25, 1997
Blood runs down the nose of Hawks center Brent Sutter after he was accidentally struck in the eye by Dallas Stars' Pat Verbeek. Three days earlier, Sutter received 25 stitches around his mouth when he was sliced by a skate. Sutter played with the Hawks for seven seasons during the '90s.

IT'S ALL A BLUR. PHOTOS BY BOB RINGHAM.

THE BULLS CHAMPIONSHIP RUN WENT SO QUICKLY, IT SEEMS LIKE ONLY A DREAM NOW. PHOTOGRAPHER BOB RINGHAM DOCUMENTED THE BULLS IN MOTION DURING THE TEAM'S FINEST REGULAR SEASON, 1995-96, WHEN THE BULLS FINISHED 72-10. "I USED LONG SHUTTER SPEEDS IN AN ATTEMPT TO CAPTURE THE HIGH-SPEED ACTION ON THE COURT," HE SAID. "I WANTED PEOPLE TO GET A FEEL OF THE GAME." ABOVE, DENNIS RODMAN TOSSES HIS SHIRT INTO THE CROWD AFTER BEING EJECTED FROM A GAME. RIGHT: RODMAN AND MICHAEL JORDAN GO UP FOR A REBOUND. FOLLOWING PAGES: SCOTTIE PIPPEN MAKES A LAYUP, AND MICHAEL JORDAN DRIVES THE LANE. IT WAS THE GREATEST TEAM IN NBA HISTORY.

'OLD GIRL' BIDS ADIEU.
PHOTO BY TOM CRUZE,
MARCH 24, 1994
A CHICAGO STADIUM EM-
PLOYEE SWEEPS OUT THE
STADIUM AFTER THE LAST
REGULAR-SEASON BULLS
GAME PLAYED THERE. THE
BULLS AND BLACKHAWKS
MOVED TO THE UNITED CEN-
TER BEFORE THE START OF
THE NEXT SEASON.

SCENES FROM SIX CHAMPIONSHIPS. 1991, 1992, 1993 AND 1996, 1997, 1998
TOP ROW FROM LEFT: MICHAEL JORDAN (PHOTO BY TOM CRUZE.), NORTH SIDE STREET CELEBRATION (PHOTO BY JOHN FREIDAH.), AND JORDAN WINS SECOND TROPHY (PHOTO BY PHIL VELASQUEZ.) SECOND ROW: HORACE GRANT (PHOTO BY RICH HEIN.), NORTH SIDE BAR FANS (PHOTO BY ERNIE TORRES.), AND SCOTTIE PIPPEN. (PHOTO BY JON SALL.) BOTTOM ROW: JORDAN AS BASEBALL PLAYER (PHOTO BY TOM CRUZE.), JORDAN WINS FOURTH (PHOTO BY TOM CRUZE.), AND DENNIS RODMAN. (PHOTO BY BRIAN JACKSON.)

TOP ROW: JORDAN CAN'T BELIEVE IT (PHOTO BY PHIL VELASQUEZ.), RON HARPER (PHOTO BY ELLEN DOMKE.), AND JORDAN WINS FIFTH. (PHOTO BY ROBERT A. DAVIS.) SECOND ROW: JORDAN FACES FANS (PHOTO BY NANCY STUENKEL.), LUC LONGLEY HUGS STEVE KERR (PHOTO BY ROBERT A. DAVIS.), AND PIPPEN BUOYS JORDAN. (PHOTO BY TOM CRUZE.) BOTTOM ROW: SOUTH SIDE FAITHFUL, (PHOTO BY SCOTT STEWART.), PHIL JACKSON (PHOTO BY JON SALL.) AND FAN GUTHRIE BONNETT. (PHOTO BY JOHN H. WHITE.)

BULLS BAPTISM.
PHOTO BY AL PODGORSKI,
JUNE 18, 1996
BULLS FANS ARE SPRAYED
BY FIRE HOSES AT THE
GRANT PARK RALLY THAT
MARKED THE RETURN OF
CHAMPIONSHIP BASKET-
BALL TO CHICAGO. ABOUT
250,000 CHICAGOANS
GREETED THE BULLS AF-
TER THE TEAM BEAT THE
SEATTLE SUPERSONICS
TO BRING THE TROPHY
BACK AFTER A TWO-YEAR
ABSENCE.

PAYTON'S PLACE.
BEARS RUNNING BACK WALTER PAYTON ANNOUNCES FEBRUARY 2, 1999, THAT HE HAS A RARE LIVER DISEASE THAT WILL LEAD TO LIVER FAILURE UNLESS HE RECEIVES A TRANSPLANT. "YEAH, I'M SCARED," PAYTON SAID. "BUT IT'S NOT IN MY HANDS ANYMORE; IT'S IN GOD'S HANDS." PAYTON FOUND OUT IN MAY THAT HE HAD A MALIGNANT TUMOR, WHICH PRECLUDED A TRANSPLANT. HE DIED NOVEMBER 1. (PHOTO BY RICH HEIN.) RIGHT: BILL STONE, OF SUBURBAN BURBANK, FIGHTS BACK TEARS AT THE WALTER PAYTON MEMORIAL SERVICE AT SOLDIER FIELD ON NOVEMBER 6. (PHOTO BY TOM CRUZE.)

A NEW BEARS DEN.
BEARS LINEBACKER BRIAN URLACHER CHECKS OUT THE NEW SOLDIER FIELD AT THE TEAM'S FIRST NIGHT PRACTICE ON SEPTEMBER 18, 2003. (PHOTO BY TOM CRUZE.) LEFT: FANS AND THE BEARS CELEBRATE THE OPENING OF THE NEW $600-MILLION STADIUM ON SEPTEMBER 29. THE CELEBRATION DIDN'T LAST LONG. THE BEARS LOST THE OPENER TO THE—WHO ELSE?—GREEN BAY PACKERS. (PHOTO BY JON SALL.)

THROUGH A GLASS SWIFTLY. PHOTO BY JEAN LACHAT, FEBRUARY 25, 2004
EXERCISE RIDERS AND JOCKEYS TAKE TO THE HAWTHORNE RACE COURSE TRACK IN SUBURBAN STICKNEY,
THREE DAYS BEFORE THE START OF THE RACING SEASON. THE RETURN OF THOROUGHBRED RACING HAS
LONG BEEN A HARBINGER OF SPRING. WROTE SUN-TIMES REPORTER JIM O'DONNELL: "BE IT EVER SO IN-
DUSTRIAL, THERE'S NO PLACE LIKE HAWTHORNE FOR THE MAINSTREAM HORSEPLAYER IN CHICAGO."

In the money. Photo by Bob Ringham, June 12, 1990
Kentucky Derby winner Unbridled parades down the paddock at Arlington Park on his way to his summer home. The track hosted the world's first million-dollar thoroughbred turf race, known as the Arlington Million, in 1981. Four years later, fire gutted the original race track, but the "Miracle Million" was held in front of 25,000 fans using temporary facilities 25 days later. The new Arlington reopened in 1989.

OFF TRACK. PHOTO BY JOHN J. KIM, MAY 8, 2004
CALVIN HAYES, OF HUBBARD HIGH SCHOOL, RUNS TO FIRST PLACE IN THE 4-BY-100-METER RELAY AT THE CHICAGO
PUBLIC HIGH SCHOOLS ATHLETIC ASSOCIATION TRACK-AND-FIELD CITY CHAMPIONSHIP AT HANSON PARK.

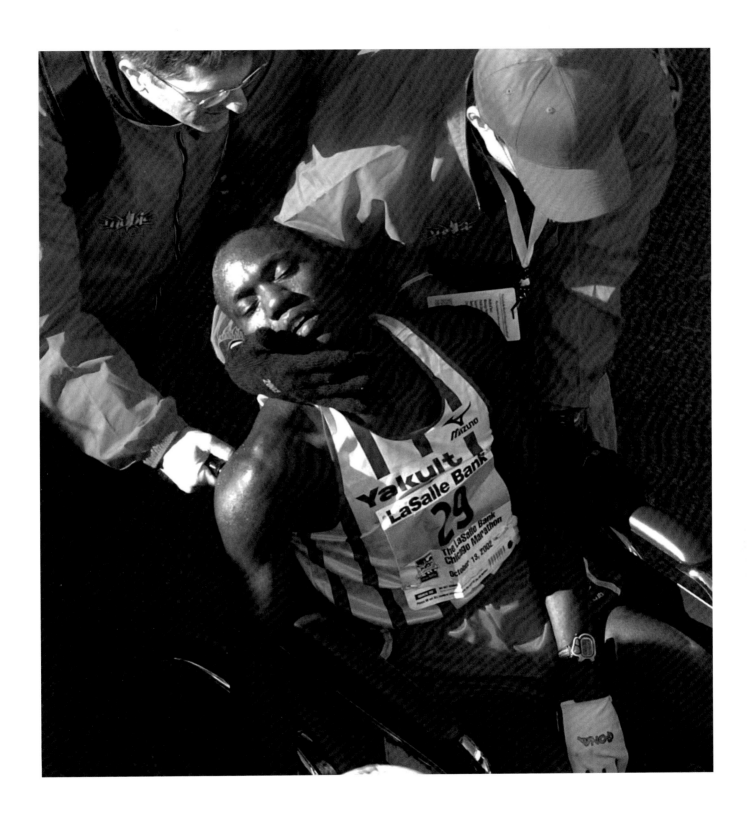

RUNNER UP. PHOTO BY JEAN LACHAT, OCTOBER 13, 2002

DANIEL NJENGA, WHO FINISHED SECOND IN THE CHICAGO MARATHON, IS TAKEN AWAY AFTER COLLAPSING AT THE FINISH LINE. NJENGA, OF KENYA, BLACKED OUT WHEN HIS BLOOD PRESSURE PLUMMETED. HE WAS RELEASED AFTER 45 MINUTES. HE FINISHED THIRD IN 2003 AND SECOND IN 2004, BUT COLLAPSED AT THE END OF THAT RACE, TOO.

IT'S REAL.
LANE TECH HIGH SCHOOL PLAYERS TOUCH THEIR CHAMPIONSHIP PLAQUE AFTER WINNING THE CITY BASEBALL CHAMPIONSHIP OVER HARLAN HIGH SCHOOL ON MAY 23, 2005, AT U.S. CELLULAR FIELD. (PHOTO BY KEITH HALE.) RIGHT: TIGER WOODS KISSES HIS TROPHY AFTER WINNING THE 81ST PGA CHAMPIONSHIP BY ONE STROKE OVER SERGIO GARCIA AT THE MEDINAH COUNTRY CLUB ON AUGUST 15, 1999. STARTING WITH THIS VICTORY, WOODS WON SEVEN OUT OF THE NEXT ELEVEN MAJOR CHAMPIONSHIPS—INCLUDING FOUR CONSECUTIVE MAJORS. (PHOTO BY TOM CRUZE.)

Expect victory. Photo by Phil Velasquez, November 4, 1995
Northwestern University cornerback Chris Martin basks in the attention that the Wildcats garnered in the team's Big Ten championship season. Martin and his teammates were introduced before taking on Penn State at Dyche Stadium. Northwestern beat Penn State for the first time, sparked by Martin's interception. The Wildcats posted a perfect Big Ten season, but lost in the Rose Bowl to the University of Southern California.

A BANNER NIGHT. PHOTO BY JON SALL, OCTOBER 12, 2002
CHICAGO WOLVES CAPTAIN STEVE MALTAIS CARRIES THE CALDER CUP INTO ALLSTATE ARENA BEFORE THE START OF THE
2002-2003 ICE HOCKEY SEASON. THE WOLVES, FOUNDED IN 1994, WON TWO CHAMPIONSHIPS IN THE INTERNATIONAL
HOCKEY LEAGUE AND THEN WON THE CALDER CUP IN ITS FIRST YEAR IN THE AMERICAN HOCKEY LEAGUE.

THIS ONE'S FOR YOU.
CUBS PLAYERS WEAR A PATCH RECALLING HARRY CARAY ON OPENING DAY AT WRIGLEY FIELD ON APRIL 3, 1998. CARAY, WHO BROADCAST GAMES FOR THE CUBS FROM 1982 UNTIL 1997, DIED BEFORE THE START OF THE 1998 SEASON. (PHOTO BY BOB BLACK.) RIGHT: PREPARATIONS ARE COMPLETED FOR JACK BRICKHOUSE'S FUNERAL AT ST. JAMES EPISCOPAL CATHEDRAL ON AUGUST 12, 1998. "HE WAS THE VOICE OF OPTIMISM," EULOGIZED BRUCE DUMONT, A BRICKHOUSE FRIEND. (PHOTO BY AL PODGORSKI.)

SLUGGERS. PHOTOS BY TOM CRUZE.

FRANK THOMAS LED THE WHITE SOX TO DIVISION CHAMPIONSHIPS IN 1993 AND 2000 DURING HIS CAREER AS ONE OF THE ALL-TIME BEST SOX HITTERS. HERE HE PLAYS AT U.S. CELLULAR FIELD ON MAY 30, 2005, A YEAR SHORT-ENED BY INJURY. RIGHT: SAMMY SOSA FLIES THE FLAG ON SEPTEMBER 27, 2001, AS HE ROUNDS THE BASES FOLLOWING HIS 59TH HOMER. IT WAS THE CUBS FIRST HOME GAME SINCE THE SEPTEMBER 11 TRAGEDY. THAT YEAR, SOSA BECAME THE FIRST PLAYER TO HIT 60 HOME RUNS IN THREE SEASONS.

EIGHT IN THE EIGHTH. PHOTOS BY TOM CRUZE, OCTOBER 14, 2003
CUB PLAYERS LOOK DOWN THE LEFT-FIELD LINE AND PITCHER MARK PRIOR POINTS AFTER CUBS FAN STEVE BART-
MAN DEFLECTED A FOUL BALL THAT MAY HAVE BEEN PLAYABLE IN GAME 6 OF THE NATIONAL LEAGUE CHAMPION-
SHIP SERIES. THE CUBS WERE LEADING 3-0 WITH ONE OUT IN THE EIGHTH INNING WHEN FLORIDA MARLINS' LUIS
CASTILLO HIT A BALL TOWARD THE SEATS IN FOUL TERRITORY. THREE WALKS, THREE SINGLES, THREE DOUBLES AND
AN ERROR LATER, THE MARLINS WON THE GAME AND WOULD TAKE THE PENNANT THE NEXT NIGHT.

STILL THE MAN. PHOTO BY JOHN J. KIM, FEBRUARY 2, 2005
MUHAMMAD ALI, WHO FIRST DIS-
TINGUISHED HIMSELF IN CHICA-
GO IN THE 1959 PAN AMERICAN
GAMES, DRAWS ON THE BLACK-
BOARD FOR CHILDREN AT AN AF-
TER-SCHOOL PROGRAM AT THE
FIRST BAPTIST INSTITUTIONAL
CHURCH. ALI DREW STICK FIGURES
SHOWING HIMSELF VICTORIOUS
OVER JOE FRAZIER. HE ADVISED
THE KIDS TO PAY ATTENTION, FIN-
ISH THEIR HOMEWORK AND STAY
OUT OF TROUBLE. "DON'T TRY TO
BE LIKE ME," HE SAID, "BECAUSE
I'M THE MAN."

THE BEST OF TIMES; THE WORST OF TIMES.
THE 2005 WHITE SOX GOT OFF TO ITS BEST START EVER IN A ROLLER-COASTER SEASON THAT ESTABLISHED THE
TEAM AS ONE OF BASEBALL'S BEST. ABOVE: A FAN WATCHES THE ACTION FROM THE OUTFIELD STANDS AT U.S.
CELLULAR FIELD ON AUGUST 16. (PHOTO BY RICHARD A. CHAPMAN.) LEFT PAGE, CLOCKWISE FROM TOP LEFT:
FIRST BASEMAN PAUL KONERKO (PHOTO BY AL PODGORSKI.), PITCHER MARK BUEHRLE (PHOTO BY RICHARD A.
CHAPMAN.), CENTER FIELDER AARON ROWAND (PHOTO BY AL PODGORSKI.) AND DESIGNATED HITTER CARL EV-
ERETT. (PHOTO BY JOHN J. KIM.)

ACKNOWLEDGMENTS

Once again, the authors would like to thank the *Chicago Sun-Times* for the use of its photographs, and for its trust and support in the creation of this book. We would like to particularly thank publisher John Cruickshank, who believes in the power of photography, and Keith Hale, who originated the idea for this book. "More than anything else, Chicago loves sports," he said.

Most important thanks go to the photo staff of the *Chicago Sun-Times*, especially the photographers who do the day-to-day work covering every major sporting event in the city. What sounds like a glamorous job is also a physically demanding, difficult one, which takes the utmost of skill, patience and ability. Special thanks should be given to Nancy Stuenkel, photo editor of the paper, who made us feel at home, and to Ron Theel, Herb Ballard and Virginia Davis, who once again opened the archive. Former photographers Bob Ringham, Fred Stein, Jack Lenahan and Bob Kotalik directed us to hidden gems. Also providing assistance were John Barron, Don Hayner, Deborah Douglas, Toby Roberts, Ernie Torres, Dom Najolia, Jim Fleming, Linda Loye, Jaclene Tetzlaff, Dan Miller, Robb Montgomery, Eric White, Tom McNamee, Jim Kirkpatrick, Albert Dickens, George McCaskey, Roger Feldman, Joel L. Hecker and *Sun-Times* sports editor Stu Courtney and his staff.

First printing: October 2005

Edited by Richard Cahan, Michael Williams and Neal Samors.

Produced by Michael Williams.

Book designed by Michael Williams and Richard Cahan.

Printed in Canada by Friesens Corporation.

ISBN: 0-9725456-5-4 (Softcover)

ISBN: 0-9725456-6-2 (Case)

Front Cover: Gale Sayers at Wrigley Field, November 27, 1967. (Photo by Gary Settle.)

Back Cover: Close play at first base in Wrigley Field, May 19, 1947. (Photo by Charles Gekler.)

Frontispiece: Joe Louis reads the *Daily Times*, June 28, 1937.

Reprints of the photographs contained in this book are for sale at www.suntimes.com